BLIND
THE
SECOND
TIME

A STORY ABOUT OVERCOMING HARDSHIP AND LOVING
"TILL DEATH DO US PART"

BY HARRY FOOTNER
WITH
LARRY R. HUTSON

NORTH DAKOTA

I don't know if we lived on a farm as farmhands or if my parents actually ran the farm. We lived on two different places, the Ketchum and the Darling farms.

It seems to me that all the people out there were Swedes. Most of the men I remember chewed tobacco, and they all spit. Have you ever seen a Shitepoke take off to fly? It's a big, big, bird... like a goose. Every time they take off they shit a big long stream. That's the way those guys spit. Just like a Shitepoke taking a crap.

I remember being in the field during the time they were threshing wheat. That must have been pretty much the main crop at that time out there, or at least that's the one I remember. They had four or five teams in the field with hayracks behind. They'd pitch the bundles of grain into the hayrack and when it was full, they'd move it up by the separator, a big thing that separated the straw from the wheat. When one hayrack was empty they'd go get another one.

The separator was powered by a steam engine that was fired by a guy tending it, with coal or wood. I don't remember which. Probably wood. Funny, I don't remember any woods around in that area. I'm sure there was, but I don't remember it.

There was a big, long belt in between the steam engine and the separator. Tick-tick, tick-tick. I can just hear that dumb thing.

There would be 6 or 8 men helping, maybe 10. All the neighbors threshed together and had fun doing it. They probably drank during that time too, but I didn't get in on any of that!

It seems to me I was the only kid out there. I don't know how come they allowed it, but I was there.

Note for Librarians: a cataloguing record for this book that includes Dewey Decimal Classification and US Library of Congress numbers is available from the Library and Archives of Canada. The complete cataloguing record can be obtained from their online database at:
www.collectionscanada.ca/amicus/index-e.html
ISBN 1-4120-4591-6
Printed in Victoria, BC, Canada

TRAFFORD

Offices in Canada, USA, Ireland, UK and Spain
This book was published on-demand in cooperation with Trafford Publishing. On-demand publishing is a unique process and service of making a book available for retail sale to the public taking advantage of on-demand manufacturing and Internet marketing. On-demand publishing includes promotions, retail sales, manufacturing, order fulfilment, accounting and collecting royalties on behalf of the author.
Book sales for North America and international:
Trafford Publishing, 6E-2333 Government St.,
Victoria, BC v8t 4p4 CANADA
phone 250 383 6864 (toll-free 1 888 232 4444)
fax 250 383 6804; email to orders@trafford.com
Book sales in Europe:
Trafford Publishing (uk) Ltd., Enterprise House, Wistaston Road Business Centre,
Wistaston Road, Crewe, Cheshire cw2 7rp UNITED KINGDOM
phone 01270 251 396 (local rate 0845 230 9601)
facsimile 01270 254 983; orders.uk@trafford.com
Order online at:
www.trafford.com/robots/04-2399.html

10 9 8 7 6 5 4 3 2

CONTENTS

FORWARD	5
ORIGINS	7
NORTH DAKOTA	11
THE TARPAPER SHACK	15
SUDDEN ORPHANS	25
LIFE AFTER LOSS	29
THE ACCIDENT	39
CIVILIAN CONSERVATION CORP	43
OUT OF SIGHT	51
LEARNING TO BE BLIND	55
LIFE BEGINS	63
ROMANCE!	65
LYDIA'S YOUTH	69
THE BETROTHAL	73
MAKING A LIFE	77
AUTOMATIC ELECTRIC	83
BLIND NO MORE	85
WINE MAKING AND CANNING	89
DAY-TO-DAY LIFE	91
JUST THE WAY YOU ARE	101
THE END IN SIGHT	103
BLIND THE SECOND TIME	105
PEOPLE IN MY LIFE	135
ACKNOWLEDGMENTS	137
APPENDIX	139

FORWARD

My wife, Lydia and I had 60 years together. I finally caught up with her after two years of romancing her, and we were married, June 12, 1943. We celebrated our 58th wedding anniversary in 2001. She passed away July 20, so I had her in tow for 60 wonderful years. Sixty wonderful, super, super years. My words are kind of clumsy, but I want to dedicate this effort to her. My Lydia.

Our life was so great it seems unreal!

I have two reasons for telling my story. It is first to let everyone know something about my life with Lydia, and secondly, to say something about the handicap of being blind. Maybe it will help someone in the same predicament to see that you can do *anything* if you want to do it badly enough.

MY FATHER, RICHARD FOOTNER, C. 1924

ORIGINS

Grandpa Footner, Harry Footner, Sr. was the son of Richard Footner. The names Richard and Harry alternated for many, many generations. My grandpa Harry, and his brothers Reginald, Steven, and Francis, and a sister, whose name I don't remember, were born in Andover England. Four boys and a girl.

Reginald settled in New Zealand, Steven in Vancouver, British Columbia, and Francis who they called "Frank", and their sister, stayed in England.

I had connections with the daughter of Grandpa's sister. Her name was Molly. Molly was married to an Episcopal minister named Du Boe. They lived at Brushford Rectory in Dulverton, Somerset, England. Frank moved to Dulverton in his old age, probably to be close to his sister and to Molly. Molly had one daughter, Patsy, and I think Patsy was just a little younger than I am.

Grandpa Footner went to a boarding school in Andover. He sang in a boy's choir somewhere there. A cousin informed me that it was the Westminster Cathedral Choir.

Grandpa came to the USA as a young man and settled at St. Clair, Minnesota, a small town southeast of Mankato about 12 miles. At that time, the whole area was thousands and thousands of acres of wooded land, with a meadow here and there in the woods. They spent much of the time cutting wood and blasting out stumps, digging rocks, and anything and everything to clear the land to be tilled for crops. You'd never know it nowadays, boy. Every inch of that land out there, except the lagoons that couldn't be tilled, is farmland now. Just unreal!

The Indians were prominent at that time. In fact, St. Clair, prior to being called St. Clair, was the Winnebago Agency. I don't know if it was a compound to protect the settlers from the Indians or if it was just a place where business was conducted and what-have-you.

Grandpa married Charlotte Caldwell. She had a sister, Lidy, and a brother, George. George and his wife ran the hotel in St. Clair. I don't remember anything at all about Lidy.

Grandma's mother was born in St. Clair. Her husband, Pearson Caldwell, died and she remarried a fellow by the name of Alney who was also native to that area.

I don't really remember my mother's parents. His name was Ole Hanson and hers was Mary. They were Norwegian. We made a trip to Pray, Wisconsin in the Model T, a 1916 job, I guess probably in 1924 or 1925 to see Grandpa and Grandma Hanson. I'm pretty sure they lived in a log cabin, and I remember that we slept in the loft on a feather tick, a great big tick or pillow stuffed with feathers. I suppose there were four of us kids sleeping up there in the loft. That was the only time I ever saw them. In fact, I'm not sure now if my mother's dad was even there. He may have been dead by then. I remember Grandma had sour cream and sugar on homemade bread and I thought I was in heaven eating that stuff. That's dang near the only thing I remember about them. One of my mother's brothers never married and he lived with Grandma Hanson. She also had one of the girls of my mother's sister who had disappeared. Her sister's name was Gena Erickson.

I remember we made one trip in the Model T to Mankato too, to visit my father's parents. We always talked about having 19 flat tires on that trip. But in those days they'd jack it up, take it off, pull the inner tube out and patch it, pump it up and stick it on again. No fuss, no muss. I'm sure we had everything in the book piled in that car. It was quite an adventure.

Grandpa and Grandma Footner had four kids, all born at St. Clair. Beatrice was the oldest. Maude was second. Richard, my dad, was third, and Daisy was the fourth child.

They all took off as soon as they were old enough, and they didn't have to be very old either, in those days. I would bet my dad took off when he was 15,16,17,18... somewhere in there.

They were all educated in St. Clair. Beatrice, who we called "Aunt Trixie", went to the teacher's college in Mankato (They called it the Normal in those days.) and she became a teacher. She moved to Havana, North Dakota and taught school out there. She married Jeff Johnson and they had two kids, Evanell and Duane.

Maude moved to Mankato and married Peter Nelson. They lived just a few houses from where I live today. They had six kids. Charlotte, Ruth, Jack, Mavis, Petra and Phyllis.

Daisy went to a bookkeeping school in Mankato, Minnesota, then moved to Morgan and worked in a bank there. She married Eli Lamp who was an implement and car dealer in Morgan. They had one son, Frederick. They came often to see Grandma after Grandpa died.

My dad worked in Minneapolis and that's where he and my mother, Mattie Hanson, were married. I was born June 19, 1914 in Minneapolis. My parents were young kids, really. We must've lived in Minneapolis a couple of years and then we moved to Havana, North Dakota, I'm sure, to be near Aunt Trixie and Uncle Jeff. We farmed there for four, or maybe five years.

RICHARD (1891-1926) AND MATTIE (1890-1926) FOOTNER, C. 1913

We drank water out of a big crock water jug that was common to everyone. They wrapped a gunnysack around the jug and I suppose dunked it in the water tank, and then stuck it under a shock of wheat. That was a kind of refrigeration they had then, cooling by evaporation. I suppose I ate lunch with the men too, you know. A big shot!

We were in North Dakota during the 1918 flu epidemic. Everybody was running and hiding. They didn't want to contact anybody, but I remember my mother going to a neighbor's place and taking care of the woman.

In the summertime we traveled to Havana from the farm, in a surrey with a yellow fringe on top. It seems to me that buggy had side curtains too. If it had side curtains, I imagine it had a windshield that could be snapped, or tied on. It was drawn by a horse. I don't think they pulled it with a team, just a single horse.

I remember going to town to see the Chautauqua, a medicine show. That was a big deal in those days. They'd have a vaudeville act, or two or three. They might have a sleight of hand artist, or a dancer... an almost naked woman, or all kinds of acts they'd perform.

In between the acts, there would be a guy that would go out and hustle the crowd with an elixir that would cure everything: warts, ingrown toenails, coughs, and lumbago. You name it. It would cure it! Same as you hear on the radio today. They've got stuff that'll cure everything!

There was no charge to attend the shows. They made their money on the sales. They had pretty good crowds, as I remember, too. They sure sold stuff! People kind of appreciated the show. You stood out in front of the stage, or collapsed from standing, I suppose.

My brother, Richard, and sister Daisy were born during the time we lived in North Dakota.

I remember pretty well that when I was seven, my dad hit a rock while he was plowing and was pitched off the plow. He apparently whacked his head a good one and must have had some kind of a blood clot or some kind of injury to the brain (they said he had a stroke) because he limped after that; kind of dragged a foot.

I would guess that we moved back to the Twin Cities soon after that. We put all of our belongings in a boxcar and the three of us kids and Mother and Dad, climbed into the boxcar too, and we rode to the Cities that way. I've heard since, that was not an uncommon way of traveling, that others had done it too. Fat chance of doing that kind of travel nowadays!

I don't remember any part of that trip. We probably sat on the edge of the door with our feet hanging out! Mother and Dad didn't fuss about us, really. Like Lydia said later, she always felt her folks thought there was more where that one came from!

We landed in the Cities and my dad worked for a moving company, Boyd Movers, when we first hit Minneapolis. A short time later, he went to work for the Ford Company, downtown, building Model T Fords. If I remember right, the plant was close to the parade grounds.

Later, they built a new assembly plant in St. Paul, along the Mississippi River. To get to the plant from the Minneapolis side, we went to Fort Snelling across the bridge and then came up along the river to the plant. I don't remember how many years he worked there, but it must have been five years, or something like that.

I'm sure it wasn't too long after we landed in the Cities that Mother and Dad bought a piece of property in South Minneapolis. 5244 37th Avenue South. It was a full sized city lot, probably 50 or 60 feet wide by 150 feet deep. Some guy that owned it had a basement dug and cement blocks laid up, and behind that was a tarpaper shack. That was our home.

OUR FAMILY: DICK, MOTHER, ME, FATHER, TOM AND
DAISY. THIS MUST HAVE BEEN TAKEN JUST BEFORE
THEY DIED, 1926.

THE TARPAPER SHACK

I don't know how much they paid for it but I remember hearing something about $700. Maybe that was what Auntie got for it when she sold it later to pay for the funerals.

It actually was wrapped in black tarpaper. I don't think several layers of it either. It had laths holding the tarpaper on. I can see those dumb things nailed vertically all around. The floor was wood on top of 2X4's that lay on the ground, so I'm sure it was a pretty balmy spot in the wintertime, although I really don't remember that we suffered with it.

Another thing I remember; there was a rat, in fact two times, a rat got in. One time it got in the wall. There was kind of an inner wall to this shack and they had to take one of the boards off to get the dumb thing out. They did the same thing when one got under the floor, and that's how I saw how the floor was built.

We had a 1916 Model T Ford, and we had a shelter to put it in. It wasn't much of a shelter but I guess it kept *some* of the snow and ice off of it.

There was a pump out by the front door where we drew the water.

There were two bedrooms and a living room/dining room/kitchen, all in one, where we did all our living. I remember some of the stuff that was in the house. There was a cook stove that Mother cooked on, that was fired with coal or wood. It had a warming oven above for toast and stuff, to keep things warm after they had been cooked. It was kept warm by the heat coming up from the stove surface you cooked on.

There was a kerosene stove too, a two-burner job. I imagine they cooked on it in the summertime to eliminate some of the heat in the house.

We heated the house with a big, round potbellied stove in the middle of the living room. That was fired with wood, or coal when we could afford it. I know that as kids we picked up every piece of wood that laid loose, and dragged it home.

We had a dining room table with chairs for all of us, and an old phonograph, a gramophone. The gramophone was one of those that had long, round, cylinder type records. You cranked it up till the spring was tightened up and then set the needle on the track on the record and listened to it squawk. I'm sure it was a horrible sound really, compared to nowadays.

They were kind of heavy and kind of squawky, but they did entertain.

We didn't have a phone or electricity. We had kerosene lamps and one of those gas mantle lights that gave off real white light. I remember we had a kerosene lamp out in the living room and one for the bedroom. They had the odor of burning kerosene, and the mantle light gave off an odor too, of burned gasoline or whatever they used. Some of the people along the street out there had electricity, but we didn't.

We had a crystal radio though. We'd have to find a radio station on that little crystal with a tickler, a little thing with something like a wire extending from it, that we pushed around until we heard the station at just exactly the right spot. There were no dials. It was manual, the very beginning of radio. The whole thing was maybe 14 inches long and six inches high. There was a coil of copper wire with a slide on it. I don't know how it worked but it did. We had earphones. I think they took them apart so there were two. I suppose everybody fought to have an earphone so they could hear the radio. I'm sure there was a scramble.

There was an antenna for it out in the yard; two copper wires and a lead wire that ran into the house and attached to the radio. It stretched between 10 to 15 foot poles that were made out of two 2X4's nailed together, with a crossbar on the top where the wires attached. I suppose it was 30 or 40 feet long altogether. The poles were supported by guy wires to keep them straight, something for everybody to trip over.

I don't remember much about what we'd hear on the radio, but I do remember it was the beginning of WCCO, the Washburn Crosby Company, a milling company. I think that was the only station. They started, I think, in about 1924 and I still listen to it every day.

I've listened to the sports. They have an old guy, Sid Hartman, who gives his opinion – like old guys do. I enjoy his program. It's just a five-minute deal, but he calls 'em as he sees 'em. A lot of radio personalities have grown old and retired and died, that were like old shoes. It was a super, super station, but now, to me it doesn't have the same appeal that it used to have.

There were some pretty funny personalities on radio, like Boone and Erickson, and Steve Cannon. Boone is back on Saturdays now. He's a good entertainer. He also reads for the American Foundation for the Blind. I've heard him on the local station where they read 24 hours a day.

That old crystal radio would be quite a treasure now. I don't remember any of the other people on the avenue there, having a radio.

We didn't have a pot to pee in or a window to throw it out of, but we had that kind of stuff. My mother saw that we always had a birthday party and always had presents and a cake. We were poor, but we always had birthday parties, and it was always a pleasant time for everybody.

My favorite present was a first baseman's glove I got from my mom, for my 10th birthday. I loved to play catch and that kind of stuff. I even brought that to Mankato with me after my parents died. That was about the only thing I got. I loaned that to a kid. I was probably 17 years old or more when I let him have it, and I never got it back. That glove meant an awful lot to me, but I think he didn't much care.

We always had Christmas too, with extra food. Christmas was always big time. I remember that we had a Christmas tree every year. Mother would clip candleholders onto the tree and stick candles in them. Not only that, but she lit the candles! I suppose someone should have stood by with a bucket of water in case the tree caught fire. Imagine! A tarpaper shack? Swoosh! The Christmas tree and all would be gone!

We always had Christmas presents too. Even though we were poor, Mother seemed to manage to do those things. I remember that we got a big coaster wagon one time for our gift. It was a Hudson, with about eight inch wheels and it was about four feet long with a wooden box on it. It was big! I suppose we used to get Tommy in it and pull him around. Another time we got a Flexible Flyer sled. Oh, man, was that a neat one! There was nothing like that, boy. That was top shelf! Skis. Daisy got a pair of roller skates. She has a reminder of that. She was skating on the sidewalk and tripped and fell, and knocked a part of her tooth out. She's carrying that to this day.

I took violin lessons and Daisy took dancing lessons. We were really, really poor, but it seems to me, we were a happy family.

Lydia always said, "It seemed like you guys had more than we ever had." She talked about dragging home a leftover Christmas tree, from school, that they let her have. That was the only Christmas tree she remembered having at home.

We had an outside biffy. A two-holer. I wonder how come the two holes? I don't ever remember anybody having company out there! We also had a pot with a lid on it, indoors, for if you had to go quick.

I started smoking early on. I suppose I hocked a sack of Bull Durham and cigarette papers off my dad. I could roll 'em as good as he could when I was eight or nine years old. One time I parked in the biffy and rolled me a cigarette and fired it up, and was sitting there enjoying it, and all of a sudden I saw him through the crack in the door, coming down the lane. Quick like a bunny, I dropped the cigarette down the hole and it set the paper down there on fire. It darned near burned the outhouse down! He had stored some side curtains for the Model T on a shelf up overhead, and I remember that those things got ruined in the fire. I imagine I got a butt warming on that deal. I don't think they would have let that go by. That's for sure.

Another episode on smoking: everything was field beyond 53rd Street and the weeds had grown up pretty tall. We used to go up there, crawl into the weeds and lie there and smoke. Somebody must have thrown a cigarette butt in there. I don't remember if I did it or not, but it set that field on fire and it burned almost to the airport, which was, I suppose a mile or so beyond where we lived.

I think we had a pretty normal family. I'm sure we fought over the headphones for the radio, and I know my brothers and I wrestled around; that kind of goings on, but I'm sure we were allowed to do the normal things.

The neighborhood was real neighborly. It seems like you knew everyone in those days. I can still name, I think, *all* the neighbors on both sides of the street at that time, *and* their kids, whether they were younger or older. You knew everyone. It was just super. I was still only 11 years old when I left there, so most of my growing up in Minneapolis was from 7 to 11.

The kids in the area were kind of a neighborhood gang. We were always playing some kind of a game. We were always active, real active. We'd play baseball out in the street. We gambled with marbles, shooting them out of the ring, and lagging to a line.

You'd draw a line and the one that got closest to it got the marble to keep. So we were gambling at probably seven or eight years old! We had names for the different marbles. The glass one was the Aggie. That was a treasure, boy! The other marbles were made of clay. The little ones we called Commies. You'd run around with a sack full of Commies.

We rolled marbles on the sidewalk too. You'd always try to get behind a high crack in the sidewalk. You'd set your Aggie up on top of the high part of the crack and then they'd roll at it from maybe a square or two away. When they rolled the marble, it would jump over the Aggie so you'd set spread legged behind the Aggie and catch all the marbles they missed with. As soon as they hit the Aggie you'd pick up and they'd sit down.

In the wintertime, we used to go to the dump and slide down toward Lake Nokomis. That'd be going west of where we lived.

People would throw their ashes and stuff out there. I'm pretty sure that's where they built Keewaydin Grade School... in that dump area. It was kind of a hole we'd dump the ashes in.

We hauled our ashes to the dump in the coaster wagon and on the sled. It was a job we kids did. There wasn't any garbage pickup in those days. You hauled all your trash, but there wasn't much of it. They didn't have tin cans and plastic jugs, and all that crap then.

We built snowmen. Big ones! We had chunks of coal for eyes, and I suppose the same for the nose and mouth. And forts. We'd make a fort and then have a snowball fight. We used to have some wicked ones with the kids in the neighborhood.

I think they did have snowplows at that time. That's the early time of automobiles, but I think most of the time you just went.

The cars of those days were higher. The wheels were bigger and they had more clearance. Cars didn't hug the ground, so you could plow through a pretty good size pile of snow, and then you also had chains you put on the tires for more traction.

My best friend lived across the street from us. His name was Wallace Murdock. He was the same age as me and he had brothers and sisters that were friends with my brothers and sister. He lived in a real nice house. We were the poor ones on the block. That's for sure. It was really terrible to live in a place like that. Nowadays they wouldn't permit it.

I remember the iceman coming by in the summertime, with the ice wagon drawn by horses. Whenever he'd stop and square up a piece of ice so it would fit in the icebox, all those chips would be on the ground. You'd dash out there and pick those babies up, rinse 'em off and have ice water.

Some iceboxes would hold 50 pounds of ice, and some only 25, and some people didn't even have iceboxes, like the Footners. We didn't have a way to keep things cool, so we had to eat everything while it was fresh, or we'd can it.

Canning was a big deal with my mother. We canned lots of stuff, especially meat. We'd kill a critter and can it. I remember that we sealed the fruit jars in a copper washtub. It had a rack in it that we'd set the fruit jars on. It seems to me we had to cook them forever, processing the meat. We did everything. Carrots and beans. Not potatoes. Potatoes were easily kept without canning. We had a cellar, just a hole in the ground, really, where we stored the stuff on shelves.

My mother was a super cook with what she had to do with, and baked lots of stuff. We were kind of self-supporting with a garden and canning.

What shopping we did, we did at the neighborhood grocery store, which was about three blocks from our house. I'd sometimes go get the things that were needed that we could afford, like a bottle of milk. I think we paid cash.

We were poor. I mean really, really poor. I don't know how much Dad made working at the Ford plant, but it was damn little.

I carried the Minneapolis Journal when we lived there. It seems to me I got either two or three cents for it.

There was a construction project I carried the paper to. Some guys were working on a big building that was the beginning of the Army hospital at Fort Snelling. They were using horses and scoops to dig the basement. They lived right on the job, in bunkhouses, and they had a big cook shack they were fed in. They'd come in for lunch and dinner. They stabled the horses there and everything.

Of course, a little kid; ragged, I'm sure; I'd go into the cook shack and the cook there would invite me to eat a meal. I had hollow legs! I'm sure they just really enjoyed pouring the food into me. I can remember bacon and eggs, and potatoes and coffee. I was probably eight or nine.

But you know, my mother let me do anything and go anyplace. I remember going on down Minnehaha Creek to the mouth, where it emptied into the Mississippi River, and I couldn't have been over eight or nine years old. We wandered along down there. You could drink the water out of the creek or the river then. It was clear as crystal.

Sometimes we went to the movies at the Lyric, which was not too far from the shack, about four or five blocks, over on 50th street and 34th Avenue. There was a little business section over there. The movies then were silent, with somebody down front playing the piano. The seats were just plain wooden ones. Nothing elaborate. I didn't see a movie with sound until quite a bit later, when I lived in Mankato.

One time Mother took me to the Pantages Theater to see a play. I don't remember what it was, but it was a kid's play, and it seems to me it was at Christmas time. We took the streetcar downtown and hustled over to the Pantages.

I went to Minnehaha Elementary School in South Minneapolis. I suppose it was six to eight blocks from where we lived, maybe 10. I finished the fifth grade there.

My youngest brother, Tom was born while we lived in the tarpaper shack. I remember my mother being pregnant with him. He was a big lug, and she was as big as a barn and miserable! He was a hunk over 10 pounds when he was born, and my mother was small.

I remember one time she and my dad went to a dance. It was a special occasion. She had on a black silk dress with red sequins on the front. Marcel hair, with big deep waves, you know? She had real black hair too. She was maybe five-foot-one or two, at the most. She had a beautiful voice. I thought she was just absolutely beautiful, the prettiest thing on earth. She was really a pretty mom.

She and another guy won a prize for dancing that night. I think my dad was kind of jealous as I remember, because she was blowing about dancing with that guy.

She never worked outside the home. In those days she did the washing on the washboard, and made homemade soap. She boiled the water in a boiler that would cover two lids on the cook stove. She really did it the hard way. She'd hang the laundry out, winter and summer, or else draped it around in the house, over chairs or what have you.

I remember though, that she was always kind of sickly.

As I got older, she used to include me in on everything. She and I used to go over to Auntie's, Mother's oldest sister, Hannah. Auntie married Jimmy Martin. She never had any kids of her own, but she adopted Mike, and when her sister, Gena Erickson, disappeared and left her husband with five kids, Auntie took one of them, Alice, and gave her a home.

Auntie lived just a few houses down from us at 5224 37th Avenue South. I can still tell you her telephone number. It was Drexel 0752. Isn't that dumb, to remember that after all these years?

Auntie used to stir up the best white cake with white frosting, so fast it was unreal. She would invite Mother and me over for cake and coffee, and they'd talk. Somehow I was included in their little round table. They'd talk pretty freely around me too, even though I was only probably 9 or 10, or maybe 11. Consequently I knew more of what was going on than most kids would. My mother had big time female troubles. She and Auntie talked about that most of the time.

Auntie had a Dalmatian dog she called Old Bob. Periodically Old Bob would come over to the shack snooping around. Mother had a big tiger tomcat. He was a *big* one! One time, Old Bob was snooping around and Old Tom climbed aboard, stuck his claws into him really good and went for a ride! I can just see him going yet, yelping with every jump. The more he'd jump, trying to shake that dumb cat off, the harder Old Tom would clamp on him, and the more he'd yip. It just tickled the life out of my mother, but of course it made Auntie madder than the devil!

My dad's hair was kind of brown. He was... well, I just don't know quite how to put it. He was a drunk, actually. Big time. He was never home.

When he was home though, I think he was pretty good to us.

I guess my dad was pretty mechanical as I reflect on it now. He built the crystal radio set we had. He putzed around with that Model T a lot, overhauling it and fixing it. He tore the whole thing down and redid bearings and everything.

Whenever he was around the Model T, messing with it, I was there too, so I knew as much about it as he did; knew all the terminology and everything. He taught me how to drive, told me what to do, you know.

One time, in the wintertime, he did his damnedest to start that stupid thing, but he couldn't get it running to go to work. I suppose he choked it too long and flooded it, and it wouldn't start.

I don't know how he got to work, but when I got home from school; I must have been, maybe 10; I went out and jacked the hind wheel up so it was off the ground, turned the key on and pulled the choke out. I cranked that sucker up and the old devil started. You had more thrust with the wheel jacked up so it would turn. That's the way they started the ornery devils in the old days when they didn't want to start. After it started, I pulled the emergency brake on and dropped it back down. I learned all that from watching my dad.

I went in and told my mother that the "T" was running, and asked her if she wanted to go and get him over at the Ford plant. She must have left the kids there in that shack while the two of us went over and picked him up. I drove. She never did. He came out and he hopped in, and I drove him home. I'm sure he was kind of pleased.

The roads on the way there and back were all gravel; gravel, and snow and ice. Top speed for the old Model T was probably 20 or 25 miles an hour! That must have been in the fall before my dad died.

My dad could sing. He really could. He had a super, super voice. And yodel! Oh, God in hell. When I picture him in my mind, I see him singing. He was always doing it. He knew lots of songs, too.

I remember that Mother finally talked him into going to the Methodist church. The preacher lived right across the street and a little way north of us. He was welcomed with open arms there because he *could* sing. In fact, all of us could sing. I know I had a good voice then too. I don't remember singing a lot as a family, though. Our family ended when we were pretty young.

SUDDEN ORPHANS

——

It was April and May of 1926 when the folks died. Dad was working at the Ford plant when he had a stroke, was hospitalized and died on April 21. I think his funeral took place in a funeral home. I'm sure it was a very simple, small funeral, with just a couple of neighbors. We took him to Mankato and buried him in Glenwood Cemetery near where Grandpa and Grandma Footner are buried.

There's a Mausoleum there. His grave is to the left side of the Mausoleum, way toward the back and over to the left. I remember the people that I rode with to Mankato. It was my friend Wallace's family that lived across from us on 37th Avenue. Wallace's dad's name was Chester. Chet Murdock.

We went back to Minneapolis, and Mother decided to go to the hospital and have surgery done. I'm reasonably sure she had a hysterectomy because I was there when she talked to Auntie about the things that were wrong. I'm sure she was in hopes she'd get fixed up and would be able to take care of us one way or another.

I remember her telling Auntie, "Be sure and take care of the kids."

She went to the hospital and either died on the operating table or got an infection, and died May 9, 18 days after my dad did.

We buried her in Mankato near where my dad is buried, and went back to Minneapolis again.

Lydia always was able to walk right to the graves. Lydia and I did visit their graves periodically, not over and over and over, but we kind of kept track.

I'm sure that we stayed in that shack alone. I know when Mother went to the hospital we did. They all figured I was big enough to take over, and I did. I was 11. Daisy was probably eight or nine. Dick was seven, and Tom was four or five. I can remember those kids balling and whining for their mother. And I remember playing that dumb phonograph, trying to quiet them down. They finally did, and I crawled into bed too.

I'm sure the whole thing fell on Auntie to do. I suppose she was more or less in charge because she lived so close. The neighbors helped some. People brought in food, and stuff like that.

It must have been devastating for the people that were involved, that something like that would happen. Four little kids. Nobody wanted us, really. Not really. It was a tough time. Where to go? Where to put us?

It was a hard life when we were kids. I'm the only one that really knows. Daisy, and Dick and Tom were just little kids. I wasn't much more than a little kid when it all happened. It wasn't Easy McGee. That's for sure.

Auntie took Dick and I to a place; I'm pretty sure it was in downtown Minneapolis, around Loring Park, or right on the edge of downtown. It was a godforsaken hole. It was like a halfway house or a holding house where they'd take kids until something was done. It seems to me that we laid on the floor on a blanket. I don't think it was a mattress or anything. It was terrible. The food was even worse. We had oatmeal and I don't think there was anything else with it. No sugar. No nothing.

The next morning, I took Dick by the hand and the two of us left the joint. We didn't want any part of it. We wandered around downtown or wherever, you know. No place to go and nothing to do. They found us and hauled us back, I'm sure, with a lecture. We spent the night there again, and it was so bad that the next morning came and I did the same thing. I took Dick and we hustled out of there. That day we were out until; I don't think it was completely dark, but close; wandering around downtown Minneapolis. They picked us up again and hauled us back to the joint.

I'm sure they called Auntie and said they couldn't handle me, and that it was her problem, and they hauled us back out to her. I'm sure that really lit the fire for her. That put everybody in action to get something done.

They called Aunt Daisy and Uncle Eli to come and get Daisy. They didn't want her, but they came to Minneapolis and took her to Morgan. She really got the bad end of the stick. She never *felt* wanted. She always felt they did finally just take her to baby-sit their son, Frederick. She had a miserable life, really. She had to wear old lady clothes and old lady shoes. One time they went on vacation and left her home alone. Snuck away on her, you know? It was shitty to say the least.

Auntie took my brother Dick and raised him.

George and Genevieve Stone adopted Tom. Genevieve was a principal of Whittier Elementary School in South Minneapolis. I don't know if Whittier still exists or not. I've heard the name, but I don't know if they use the building for school or for something else. Many of the old schools have been torn down up there.

The Stones had a beautiful home at 1450 West Minnehaha Parkway, just a block from Lake Harriet. George Stone, Tom's dad, was a nice guy.

Auntie and Mike hauled me to Mankato, bundled me up with all my worldly possessions. I think the only thing I had was my first basemen's glove that I'd gotten for my 10th birthday. I suppose they dumped me off at Grandpa and Grandma Footner's and said, "Here he is. You can take care of him. See you later."

My situation was different than Daisy's though. Grandpa and Grandma Footner were very, very, very good to me, and I never felt unwanted.

ME AROUND AGE 12. THE PHOTO TAKEN BY GRANDPA FOOTNER, 1926.

LIFE AFTER LOSS

I came to Mankato and went to sixth grade at the Union School, about three blocks from Grandma and Grandpa's. Pretty handy.

That was the first time I'd had indoor plumbing or electricity. We had telephone too. It was a party line. Grandma called Aunt Maude every day and chinned with her. You'd pick up the phone and say, "Operator?" An operator answered the phone when you took the receiver off the hook, and she'd ask for the number. You gave her the number and she apparently plugged it in, and made the hookup.

The first thing, Grandpa bought me a bicycle. I loved that thing and really treasured it. We lived up over Wagon's Meat Market, on Front Street. Our address was 211 1/2 North Front Street, only about a block from where Grandpa worked at the Hubbard Milling Company. I used to haul that bike up the back steps and park it on the porch so nobody would steal the thing.

ME WITH THE BIKE GRANDPA FOOTNER BOUGHT FOR ME WHEN I CAME TO LIVE WITH THEM IN MANKATO, 1927.

That was quite an apartment. The living room was Grandma's bedroom. She had a cot out there. This room had two windows in it that looked out on Front Street, the main drag of town. There was a walk-in closet in the living room, and behind that was a kitchen. There was a bathroom in between the little dining room and kitchen, and then there was the back bedroom that Grandpa and I had our beds in.

Cockroaches used to come up the drainpipes and the water pipes. Grandma was fighting those things all the time.

Those two windows out in front provided the only ventilation in that apartment. Nothing else. I remember how hot that thing got in the summertime. It was just awful! Grandma had a little four-inch electric fan she used to blow on herself. Grandpa and I slept raw.

They used to butcher down in the back of the building too. A guy would haul a hog in there and old Charlie Wagon, the owner of the meat market, would rap him on the head and do him up. Things were different in those days.

Grandma always used to pawn me off, almost like her son. She took me everyplace when I first came to Mankato, kind of an introductory deal. She was always really, really good to me. Well, Grandpa was too. I never had any trouble with them and I never was in trouble either, big trouble anyway.

They had rules, both written and unwritten. When Grandma called, I was to come. When we lived in the Park Apartments, she'd open the window and yell. She'd scream actually. She'd go prrrrrr, screaming. I could hear her a block away, easy. That's the way she called me.

Grandpa was a real good swimmer. They said he would take a cigar and a newspaper and go out in the middle of the lake. He'd lay out there and read the paper and smoke the cigar. Of course he wasn't a showoff or anything!

He had bad teeth, so they said he pulled all his teeth with a shingle nail and a pair of pliers. He'd pry them up with the shingle nail and yank them out with the pliers. When I was living with them, one time, he had a great big lump on his belly. I suppose it was an abscess of some kind.

He got his jackknife out, sharpened it up good and sharp on a whetstone, and proceeded to cut that baby open. As I remember, it was about an inch and a half long across his belly, and maybe even longer than that. Apparently he didn't feel pain or something. I don't know. Maybe he had a couple good shots of booze before he did it.

That spring after school was out, Grandpa and Grandma thought I should go back up to the Cities to visit Auntie.

They put me on the bus to Auntie's. Of course, she had her adopted son Mike, and Alice, and my brother Dick. Well anyhow, Auntie didn't want me there. She decided it'd be a good idea if I'd go up north, so she bargained with a neighbor; Nesland was his name. They lived a door or two from the shack. He had a brother that farmed up north and they concluded that I should go up and work on the farm for the summer.

They put me on the bus and my destination was Mora, Minnesota, near Brook Park, where this brother of Nesland lived. I got to the bus depot up there and got off. There was nobody there, nobody to pick me up.

I don't know if the people at the depot called, or what the deal was, but I was stranded. Of course, not everybody had phones in those days, and Nesland didn't. What to do, you know? A 13-year-old kid, dumb in the head, that didn't know nothin', stranded at the bus depot and they didn't know what to do with him.

I think the people that ran the bus depot, kind of felt sorry for me and made some arrangements. I wound up on a farm with a young couple. I did remember their name at one time, but I don't anymore. It must have been near Brook Park.

I was on that farm two or three months, until fall. I did all kinds of farm work. I did everything, cleaned barns and cut and raked hay, curried horses. I plowed with horses, helped them thresh and the whole bag. I did pretty near everything a good farm hand would do, except, I don't remember milking. I could have, but I don't remember. I remember cleaning the milk cans and that kind of stuff.

They let me haul the cream to the creamery in a Chevrolet touring job. Uffda! That was big time for me, boy. I used to hump that baby into town with the cream can, you know. I was really livin' then. I'm sure I drove to beat hell. I had driven since I was eight years old. Now, I was 13 years old, and wheelin' and dealin'.

One night, we went to a barn dance or something, and I got crocked. I was really loaded. Staggering around, making an A-hole out of myself. But, I was a dumb kid. Not very worldly, that's for sure. I hardly knew "up".

One time, I had to go to the can and I didn't have a pot upstairs, so I peed out the window through the screen. That screen always had a big yellow mark on it!

He promised me that he would pay me, but I've still got it coming. I don't remember what he promised me, but my pay turned out to be my board and room, and a bus ticket back to Minneapolis. Period. I don't know if he said he'd send me the money or what the deal was. I always looked for it, but it never came.

You know Grandpa and Grandma were real good to me. That's for sure, but they didn't really want me either. To have somebody dumped on them? A 12-year-old kid? They hadn't had kids around for a long time. So they sent me up to the Cities. Auntie didn't want me there, so she bargained with that dude, and sent me up north, and then that guy didn't want me either.

I came back to Mankato and I did seventh and eighth grade at Franklin Junior High School. It was about 13 or 14 blocks north of where we lived.

I always went home for lunch. For sure, I didn't get lunch at school. We couldn't afford it. Everybody walked to and from school in those days, too. You didn't get bus rides. I did 9th, 10th, 11th and 12th at Mankato High School. I graduated in '33.

School was okay, I guess. I didn't hate it. I was kind of a dumb bunny, is all. I liked some parts of it. If the teachers were with it, really knew what they were teaching, I enjoyed the classes. If they were just floundering around, I could hardly stand it. I had favorite teachers. I think my favorite subject was grammar. An old lady taught it. Mary Trafton. I had her in my senior year. I suppose she was probably 60 to 65 years old, but I looked on her as a really old lady at that time. I really liked her. I learned more from her than any of them, I think. I loved history. I loved English. I loved grammar. I can still break a sentence down! I guess my least favorite subject was Latin.

After we lived at North Front, we moved into the apartments up on 4th Street. We had a basement apartment there. That was pretty nice. The layout was pretty much the same, but we had more ventilation. There was no air conditioning or any of that good stuff in those days, though. The summers were hot, and in the winters Grandma used to pound on the radiator to wake the janitor, to fire up the furnace.

All the time I lived with Grandma and Grandpa, I did the scrubbing and bathrooms and bed making. I always did all kinds of work. I honestly didn't mind doing any of that stuff. It was fun to be able to do it, I guess.

I never had sleepovers with my friends. I was a bed wetter, so I didn't venture very far. I wet the bed when I was pretty big.

I used to love to roller skate. In the late twenties, they had a roller rink in the Armory downtown. I don't know how I ever scrounged up enough money to go skating, but I did. They had the music and the whole bag. There was one girl down there in particular I used to really enjoy skating with. Helen Stewart. Funny, how a name sticks in your head. She was a good skater, and she had big boobs! That would attract a 14 or 15-year-old kid! She always wore a bright red sweater. Not the loose kind either. Get the picture?

Grandpa had a harmonica, and of course he encouraged me to play it. I was too fussy about my own playing. It was never good enough. But I remember when I was in seventh grade; Hibbard Stubbs and I were asked to play for the assembly in Franklin Junior High School. Two knuckleheads, trying to perform. It was recognizable. Oh, I can just see that twosome yet, bowing and blushing. Dumb heads!

At that time we had a streetcar that made the rounds. It kind of toured the whole town. It was fairly close to walking distance to everyone. A little Toonerville Trolley. I remember cartoon pictures of those little old streetcars. That's about the way it looked.

In those days, we didn't have any way of getting to places out of town, so we hitchhiked. You'd go out on the road, and stand and bend your thumb in the direction you wanted to go. Eventually somebody would pick you up and they'd maybe haul you all the way where you were going, if they were going that way.

All the roads were gravel yet. None paved at all. In fact the main drag in town was gravel.

We used to hitchhike out to the lakes, oftentimes, every day. Lake Washington was probably 14 miles away and Madison Lake was 12. Eagle Lake was seven or eight. It might take a couple rides to get to the lake, but we'd swim for an hour or two, and get back on the road and hitchhike home. No big deal at all.

There was a tower out on Madison Lake. It was a real high place to jump off from, into the water. I don't know, 25 feet maybe? One of the guys I was with did it. Surely, if he could, I could, and I did.

One time, Major Peek and I wanted to go to the Cities for something, and of course we didn't have any money. We thought we'd try something different, so, instead of hitchhiking, we decided to ride the rails, and caught a freight train on the fly. We had checked it out, so we knew what to do. There was a spot in behind the coal car, called the tender, the part of the steam engine that carried the coal and water. It was kind of indented there and they called it "the blinds." There was room there for us to stand or sit.

As the train was pulling out, and it was ramming along at a pretty good speed, we ran alongside. Of course, it was going a lot, lot, lot faster than we were running. Major Peek and I (Lyle Peek was his real name) grabbed on to the handrail, hung on for dear life, and swung up parallel to the tender, then moved up a couple of steps, sashayed into the blind and rode in back there, to Minneapolis.

Major Peek and I, riding the blinds.

Everyone had a nickname in those days. We called him "Major" right after he joined the National Guards. He was actually a buck Private, but we elevated him to a higher office anyhow. I did a lot with him. He was a year older than I was. We played on the same basketball team in high school.

It seems to me we went to a basketball game in Minneapolis. We probably had a dime or 25 cents. Hopping on that train was risky business. You miss, you know, and you'd be in big trouble!

One summer, when I was about 16 years old, I went to Morgan to work for Uncle Eli in the implement shop. I pumped gas. In those days, you actually pushed a handle back and forth to pump it from a tank above. You washed the windshields, and you did all that good stuff. He had the implement business and he also sold cars, both used and new. One time he wanted me to deliver a car to a guy out in the country. I delivered it all right!

I don't know if I had the gas pedal to the floor or not, but I sailed off in the ditch and I lit square with the barbed wire fence. I remember hearing those fence posts clicking off. Click, click click. Then finally I hit one and it stopped. I didn't roll the thing, and it was a fairly deep ditch too! I must have just sailed off and hit it square. Of course, dumb kid you know; I didn't know what the hell to do, but eventually somebody came along and helped. All Uncle Eli said was, "Just too damned much of your fast driving!" That was all he said to me. I don't remember how badly the thing was wrecked, but I don't think too badly.

I remember when I was 16 or 17 I was sitting on one of the benches in Washington Park. It was a real comfortable bench with a back on it and all. I was sitting there in the middle of it, and one of the younger kids (Jim Hoover) came up from behind and on impulse, locked his arms around my neck, under my chin, strangling me. There was no motive for it. It was just a dumb thing to do. He damn near killed me. I tried to poke him in the eye. I reached back and got hold of one of his ears. I did get hold of his nose one time, but I think it was the hold I had on his ear that made him finally let loose. I don't remember if I keeled over or not, but I remember it was really terrible. He was not a puny kid either. He was kind of a tough, muscular little fart.

I also remember the time that I was playing softball and I was about 10 or 15 feet away from a guy and I said, "Try to hit this one!" I wound up overhand and threw that softball, and he hit that thing, how I'll never know, and it came back and hit me in the throat. I thought I was gonna die that time too.

In high school, I played basketball with what they called the Saturday Morning League. Our team was the "Castoffs". We thought we were better than we were. That's for sure. I can still name the kids on that team. Burt Balsteader, Irv Fettke, Milt Antonson, and Ozzy Kettleson, and Harry Footner. I was the tallest, at six-foot-two, or two and a half, but not very good, that's for sure.

I did try all the sports in High School. Football, basketball, track. I made a letter in track, heaving the shot put. That was a joke. I tried to play football in Junior High School. I was never very good at any of them. I used to think I was pretty good at basketball, but really, I'm pretty sure I wasn't. Compared to these days, for dang sure I wasn't! These kids are really good now. Of course they all have their eye on a pro basketball contract with big time money, so they really get out there and bust a gut. And they're bigger, stronger, faster, and smarter.

I was a mediocre student too. I always could have done better but I was one of those smart alecs, you know? I think I ran with the wrong crowd.

We sometimes hung out at the YMCA. It was within six blocks, on the corner of 2nd and Cherry, I think, where Johnson furniture is now. We'd play basketball, go swimming, shoot pool, and play Ping-Pong. One of the first things Grandpa bought for me was a membership to the YMCA. I can still see the green card. We went to the "Y" a lot. There was always something doing there. Back then it was just for men and boys.

I never had a girlfriend when I was in school. I didn't have any money. Nothing. Zero. So, I didn't do the norm, I guess. They had school dances, but I didn't go.

When we were in high school there was a fad. We had hats they called crushers with every color of the rainbow in them. It was felt that you could crush up. That was the thing, boy, to have one of those hats.

I always parted my hair on the left side when I was a kid, and I actually had kind of a little curl up in the front. It was brown. Not dark, but kind of a shit brindle brown.

I got to drive when I lived in Mankato too. There was a guy that had a girlfriend in the Twin Cities and he had a nice new Chevrolet. He'd haul me up there, and he'd have his date, and then I'd drive him home so he could sleep. Big time chauffeur. I didn't get paid for it. Just the pleasure of driving was pay enough.

I stuck the knife in my eye my junior year in High School, which would have been in the summer of 1932. It was an accident that changed my life.

ANOTHER PHOTO OF ME TAKEN BY
GRANDPA FOOTNER, C. 1926

GRANDPA FOOTNER (1865-1936) AND ME. GRANDPA
HAD A DURHAM GRAFLEX CAMERA AND TOOK
PICTURES FOR HIS OWN ENJOYMENT. IF YOU LOOK
CLOSELY YOU CAN SEE HIM SQUEEZING THE BULB ON
THE END OF THE HOSE THAT LEADS TO THE CAMERA.
HE DEVELOPED HIS OWN PICTURES TOO, C. 1926

THE ACCIDENT

I was a part of a gang, called the Washington Park Gang, because we hung out in Washington Park. We were not a timid lot, but not the kind that roam the streets nowadays. The gangs of those days would steal cigarettes and beer, and that kind of stuff. If there was anything brewing between the gangs, they'd settle it with their fists, but not even much of that. It was just petty stuff. We didn't even really fight the other gangs. We talked about doing it, but never did. Some of those guys went on and did well.

We used to do all kinds of things in the park there. We gambled a lot. All we ever had was pennies, but we gambled. We pitched pennies to a line or shook craps, played cards, or threw a knife at a tree, or we played catch, and football and wrestled. Just all kinds of stuff that kids do, hanging out.

Going to the can was never a problem there. There was a nice big clump of bridal wreath that really seemed to thrive on urine. Now they have a big, new fancy outhouse. All the comforts of home! I'll bet we had more fun though, than the kids do now.

One of the games we played, that we were playing that day in the early summer, was baseball, with a jackknife. A lot of people think I was playing Mumbly-peg when I had my accident, but that isn't true. That's another game with a knife, but it's different from baseball.

With baseball, you needed a knife with the two blades on one end. You'd pull the short blade wide open so it was parallel with the handle and the longer blade at a right angle. You'd stick the longer blade in the ground, put your finger under the handle and flip the knife up. It would twirl around, and if it landed on the point, it was a home run. If it landed on the long blade, it was a triple. If it landed with both blades stuck in the ground, it was a double, and if it fell over, you were out. As I remember, you were allowed three outs and then the next guy would take his turn.

There were three of us playing the game. It was me, and brothers Pete and Bill Esser, both younger than me. When my turn came, as I flipped it up, my finger slid along the handle of the knife. It caught in the corner where the handle met the blade, and I hooked it into my eye.

I'm sure I cut a really good gash in the thing. You know you flip the knife with pretty good force to get it up in the air. Pete led me to the clinic, which was about three or four blocks from Washington Park. I had a tremendous burning sensation in that eye when we were walking to the clinic. In fact, it was so intense that I couldn't see out of the other one, my good eye. The doctors there started to do their thing. They got the eye cleaned up, patched and I went home. Not real good care, looking back on it and knowing what I know now. I didn't know anything then. I developed an infection and they monkeyed with it over a period of about a month or more.

Finally the infection got so bad in that eye that it started to affect my other eye, so they took the bad eye out. I went to the clinic and Grandpa came down to be with me. He waited until I was through with the operation. They gave me a good big shot of ether, laid me out and took the eye out. After the operation, I went in and slept the ether off. It seems to me it was about 3:00 or 4:00 in the afternoon when I got up from that and walked home. It wasn't very far, three or four blocks.

On the way, there was a girl in my class who lived next door to the apartments where we did. Of course I had this great big bandage over my eye, and I know it was bloody. When I went by, she saw me, and she asked me what happened. I said, "They took my eye out". I remember she got white as snow. I thought she was going to faint but she didn't. I didn't stop very long. I was anxious to get in the house.

I went to the Cities to get a glass eye. They said that Dr. Miller had done a good job removing that eye, and that it was done real well.

They have great gobs of artificial eyes, many shapes and sizes. In general, they're shaped like a shell. Those people are experienced and I suppose even by looking, they can come fairly close. They keep fitting an eye until they have one that's the right size and shape. They matched my other eye, and it was a pretty good match too.

It doesn't take much of a change to move it right or left, or up or down because it's held in by the upper and lower eye lids, and held against an egg-shaped muscle behind.

I had a glass eye for a few years. They deteriorate and you can't drop them in the sink. That's for sure. They're hollow and go into a million pieces. I dropped a couple. I don't know who paid for those. I'm sure Grandpa and Grandma didn't. I had lots of stuff like that done for me anonymously. People have always been real good to me. Everyone. That's for sure.

I have a plastic eye now that I've had for many years. Good thing, too. I've dropped it into the sink several times recently. It seems to be more difficult to get off. They do need attention. You have to clean them up, just like you would clean false teeth. I take it out and wash it. Lydia used to polish it for me occasionally. I don't know what she used.

Any little fleck of dust or anything is really irritating. It hurts! It seems to be even more sensitive than a normal eye.

I would guess it's been 30 years now since I bought my last one.

During my senior year in high school I was in the library studying (that would be questionable I suppose) and I had a book in front of me. My glass eye was watering, and I took my handkerchief, dried the tear, and bent down over the book again. Then I raised up and looked across the table at the girl across from me and she said, "Oh my God! Oh my God! What happened to you? What's wrong with your eye?"

Well, I knew right away what I'd done. When I wiped my eye, I had turned that damned thing around and I was looking out the corner. Quick like a bunny, I hopped up, dashed into the boy's can and turned that baby around so I was looking straight ahead again.

The hardest thing to get used to when I lost that first eye, was having to turn my head to see things on the side where it was removed, although

I would say, having one eye never really bothered me. Not really. I still did pretty much the same as always.

Grandpa and Grandma insisted on me finishing High School. Otherwise, I would imagine, I would have dropped out.

There must have been 100-150 in my graduating class. When I graduated, I walked up to the podium, got my diploma, and listened to some guy waste his time. I didn't do anything special. I didn't have a yearbook or pictures, invitations or anything.

I graduated from high school in 1933 and, incidentally, so did Daisy. She was 16 years old. She'd made up the grades by taking extra subjects. She went to the teacher's college here and taught for a few years.

We were in the middle of the Great Depression. It was really, really tough.

I remember shoveling snow for Mrs. Rosenburg. The Rosenburgs had a corner lot right across the street from where we lived in the Park Apartments. It had a good-sized driveway, and we had about an 8 or

10-inch snowfall. I shoveled that sidewalk and driveway clean, clean, clean, to the bone. I went up to collect my wages and she gave me a dime and a Pyramid Chocolate. It was funny I didn't tell her to take that chocolate and shove it. I wasn't above that in those days, but I ate the damned thing, I'm sure.

The depression was terrible, and long lasting too. I don't think I made 10 dollars in 1933 or 1934, to the time I went into the CCC camp.

MY SISTER, DAISY FOOTNER, C. 1936

CIVILIAN CONSERVATION CORPS

"CCC" stands for Civilian Conservation Corp, which was the Roosevelt administration's doing, maybe one of the best things that ever happened. It took kids off the street that couldn't buy a job, and put them to work. We got a dollar a day. You sent 25 dollars home, and you got to keep five dollars in camp. I think my Grandpa and Grandma pretty much lived on that 25 dollars I sent home over the time I was in there.

Every so often, I'd ask them for a little of that money and they never refused me. They'd send something. I don't remember if it was a ten spot or what, but they always sent something.

We were inducted into the CCC camp in military style at Fort Snelling, in Minneapolis. We had a physical examination there. We were put aboard the train and sent to Two Harbors, and then we all crawled into trucks and were hauled out to the campsite.

I was at a camp in the boonies, north of Two Harbors on the shore of Lake Superior, camp 2710. It's now Gooseberry State Park. It was really rough when we got there. Beautiful, beautiful country! God's country! I really enjoyed that. The Gooseberry River runs through the park. There are three waterfalls along the way to Lake Superior, where the mouth of the river is wide and open. One of the waterfalls was right close to the area where they built the barracks.

It must have been, I'd say in late May or early June when we went up there. I think we had to set up tents when we arrived. We lived in those tents for three or four months, until after the snow fell and the barracks were done and ready for us to move into.

We each had a canvas cot with a mattress on it, and we were issued clean sheets and clothes. The issue was old Army stuff. We had knickers. Oh God, we must have been a cute array of boys.

We came from all walks of life. Some of the kids' folks were pretty well off, but most of them were really off the street.

The tents had dirt floors and held about 10 or more, maybe a dozen guys. They dug a trench around the outside so the water wouldn't run in from a rain.

In the summertime, the mosquitoes were big and hungry, and there were lots of them. We had mosquito nets that would make it possible to sleep at night and not get carried away.

We drove a pole with a cross bar on top, into the ground on each end of the canvas cot. Then we draped a mosquito net over that. There were wood ticks and all the good stuff up there; bees and bugs and what have you.

I'm pretty sure the age ranged from 18 to 30. A few of the guys there had been in the Navy, the Army, and the Marines, from all branches of the service. They knew the ropes a little bit better. That's for sure. There were some guys there who were really tough, but I don't remember any real big time problem. The guys in the camp disciplined themselves.

We had leaders. Of course, they were big timers, boy. They got 45 dollars a month! The assistant leader got 36 dollars a month. That's where I landed, as assistant leader. I was just one of the boys when I first went up there. I don't know why I was picked to be an assistant leader. I don't remember the circumstances at all, but there was some decision that this guy could possibly do the job. I was an ornery devil. I know that.

I think I reflected my background, having lived with my Grandpa and Grandma. They were correct in the things they did and the way they talked. I suppose I kind of did that too. That might have been a reason for them picking me out. I don't think it was strictly merit. I think all of the promotions came out of the blue. You had no inkling it was about to happen. Actually, I think maybe they kind of did an eenie-meenie-miney-moe. The officer just looked over the crowd and picked out the ones that looked the orneriest for leaders.

There were a couple of the leaders that would take on anybody in the camp. Successfully! Nobody pushed them around.

The commanding officer and his subordinates were all Army people in uniform. The doctor was a Major. The camp commander was a Captain. He had two Lieutenants under him. We had a superintendent civilian that headed up all the work projects, and he had foremen under him.

We'd get up in the morning at seven o'clock, if I remember right. They had a bugler, Roy Brady, who blew taps at night and revelry in the morning. He could really honk that thing!

The tents were heated with little bitty heaters called Salamanders, one of those on each end of the tent. Firemen came along and poked wood into them.

They cooked outside. We had good food and lots of it. They had really, really good menus. Healthy. But the main thing was that there was plenty. They had a baker or two, a head cook, and half a dozen underlings. The cook was a great big dude. He was tall and heavy.

The food was served in a mess kit, like they had in the Army in the First World War. It was a little oval shaped aluminum dish with a handle on it. In the tents, they had a big tank of water, like they used for watering horses. After you finished eating you'd just douse your dish up and down a few times to get most of the stuff out, slap the cover on it and wait for the next meal. I don't remember anybody being sick up there to amount to anything. We had a couple guys with appendicitis, but nothing serious.

They finally finished the barracks after the snow had fallen. It was time to get into them! There must have been about 10 barracks, and about 20 or 30 guys to a barrack. It'd get pretty foul in there once in awhile.

Two Harbors was our town. We'd go there on Saturday night if we had a couple of bucks. If you didn't, you'd set tight at camp.

We were split into crews. The first thing we did was fight forest fire.

Kids were put out into the fire area with very little instructions or training. I would guess we were out at that, three or four weeks.

They just put you out there with a shovel, a mattock and a tank full of water you'd squirt on the fire. We dug trenches and built backfires. There was very little instruction. Funny nobody got hurt. We never had a fatality. There was I think, 250 guys in the camp. Nobody died in the time I was there, and I was there at least two full years, about six months of 1934, all of 1935, and a part of 1936.

While we were there, we built roads, cabins and picnic shelters, and we built the road into Split Rock Lighthouse. It looked just like a little top hat when we went up there. There was a single road going in, almost like a cow path. They manned that lighthouse with three guys, in three shifts around the clock, 24 hours a day. It had big foghorns and flashing lights. I don't know how far ships were able to see that, but I know they sure used it.

We quarried granite in Duluth. I spent a lot of time there with the gang that quarried the granite. We had an old, Italian foreman. He was a stonemason and he was really good at it. We had a big compressor out there with jackhammers. We drilled holes and stuffed dynamite into them blew the granite loose, and then hand loaded it onto a truck.

Of course the goal was always to get big pieces that would weigh somebody else down so they couldn't handle it!

It's surprising what you can do with manpower, though. All we had was a skid, two big heavy pieces of timber, about 10 feet long, or maybe even a little bit longer than that. They'd hook them onto the end of the truck. Mostly with bars, we'd skid up pieces of granite that actually almost filled the whole truck in one piece. Unreal!

It was pretty, pretty granite too, blue and red. The quarries were just on the edge of Duluth, just a little up the north shore. They used the granite to build the lower parts of the cabins, the refectory, picnic shelters, and wherever else it was needed.

I also worked with a crew that made shakes. You'd go out in the woods and harvest cedar logs. They'd bring the log back in and then cut them to the length of a shingle or shake. You had a big bar-like knife and you'd split off a piece from the log and trim it to the right shape. We had a way to pile them so they would air dry. We made thousands and thousands of shingles with a hatchet!

You had to sharpen your hatchet on a whetstone. Of course you kept that thing like a razor. Sharpening your hatchet would kill time too. You wouldn't have to do anything while you were sharpening your hatchet! We made shingles for all the buildings we built and there were lots of them.

Of course we cut wood. Wood for cooking took a lot, and wood for all the barracks. They had crews cutting, splitting and hauling wood all the time. That was a big time job. They must have had two, three, or maybe four trucks hauling wood all the time.

Wandering out in the wilds, you know, you'd see lots of wildlife. We saw deer, moose, coon, badgers, beaver, and bear. There was pretty much everything in the immediate area.

I think we worked an eight-hour day, counting travel. They trucked everybody to and from the job, and they'd bring lunch out to where we were working.

There was a doctor there available all the time. He lived in a cabin near the camp.

We had a recreation hall that had two or three Ping-Pong tables and two or three pool tables. They showed movies. They had boxing matches, between the guys from the camp and sometimes they brought guys in from other camps. I only remember one knock down, drag out fight when two guys got at each other for something. The officers made them put gloves on and let them go at it. One of them finally beat the other one down. There was a ring around them and everyone watched with much joy, I suppose, while some guy beat hell out of another one. I only remember that happening one time during the time I was there.

The kids used to spend lots of hours down on the shore of Lake Superior, especially around the mouth of the Gooseberry River. It was real sandy down there and it was a good source for agates. I never found a very big one. I had a pint jar, about half full of them, and I had a ring made for our daughter, Mary from a moss agate I found down there.

There was a guy named Henderson, and his wife, that lived in the woods. I got to be friends with him. I don't know if he got a job working for the camp or what. Anyhow, he invited another guy and I, to come over to his place for a weekend, so we went over and stayed with them.

We decided to go out and explore the area, and got lost. We walked and walked and walked, for I don't know how long, and came up on our tracks again. We had just been going in a circle. We did find our way out of it, eventually.

I always talked about Henderson, and one time when Lydia and I were up north of Two Harbors, we went to see the old Henderson house. It was dilapidated and just a pile of nothing, rotted away. Lydia dug a pine tree and brought it home. We have the Henderson pine in our backyard right now. It's the pine tree closest to the shed out in back. I venture, it's 30 to 40 feet high.

In the winter of '36, my left eye started going bad. It got progressively worse. They sent me to the hospital in Duluth. They didn't want me there, so they sent me back to camp.

It was kind of dumb. I couldn't see to read. Grandma had written a letter to me and I was too embarrassed to have anybody read my mail. Stupid or not, that's the way it was. She had written in that letter, that I should come home, because Grandpa had died March 20. I never did have the thing read. Finally they called on the telephone to tell me that I should come home, and I did. I couldn't see very well. That's for sure.

I took the train to Minneapolis, and was walking across the lobby of the depot, when a woman came up to me and asked if I was Harry Footner. I said I was, and she said, "Well, I'm your Aunt Trix." I'm sure she hadn't seen me, nor I her, from the time I was seven years old. I was in my twenties then.

She said, "I knew you by the way you walk. You walk just like your dad." I rode to Mankato from Minneapolis with her. We buried Grandpa at Glenwood Cemetery, and I went back up to camp.

They sent me to Fort Snelling Army Hospital in Minneapolis. The Army Hospital then, was quite different from the Army Hospital now. There were old Army vets in there, you know. They had been through the mill and were really tough. And with a punk kid comin' in you know? The nurses were tough too!

I had lots of pain. I suppose that was the reason I finally went to the doctor. I had so much pain with it. Well, I was in there and *they* were anxious to get rid of me too. They didn't want any blind guy on their shoulders. So, they mustered me out of the CCC's.

I didn't have anything to fall back on. I went back to Mankato and to Grandma.

ME AT CAMP 2710, GOOSEBERRY FALLS,
MN, CCC'S, 1934

GRANDMA CHARLOTTE CALDWELL FOOTNER
(1865-1947), C. 1946

OUT OF SIGHT

There were people in Mankato that knew of my problem and they wanted to do something. I'm sure they bullied the eye specialist to see what he could do. A lady named Nina Pepper hauled me back and forth to his office many, many times. Her husband worked at the Hubbard Mill where my Grandpa did. They had an eight or nine-year-old daughter that was autistic, so I think Mrs. Pepper had a soft spot in her heart for people that had big problems.

My sight got progressively worse. Then Mrs. Stone, who had adopted my brother Tom, came to Mankato and took me back to her house. I lived with the Stones, I would guess, the bigger part of a year. I'm sure she browbeat Arthur Edward Smith, who was a renowned eye specialist, into taking me on. During the time I was there, I had lots of surgeries, little ones and big ones. I had lots of what they called "needlings". I don't know what they did, exactly. They stuck a needle into my eye and drew something out.

I had an operation called the Horner External Iridectomy. They cut a moon-shaped flap in my eye, raised it up and I guess they cut adhesions loose.

I had a tonsillectomy. They must have thought since I had an infection in the eye, maybe the tonsils were giving me a problem, so they took them out.

Mrs. Stone and her husband George had to work, and Tom was in school, so they took me down and I had the tonsillectomy and went right back to the house. They brought brother Dick over to be my nurse. He was dumb, and I was dumber. I started to bleed big time, and I swallowed an enormous amount of blood. I did make it to the bathroom and threw up. It's funny I didn't bleed to death, 'cause I didn't know what to do, and for sure Dick didn't.

I think I could see a little bit yet at that time. It seems to me that the last thing I saw was Thanksgiving dinner. Mrs. Stone's stepbrother and his wife and family had invited us over for Thanksgiving. I saw the food on the plate. I had surgery the next day, and I've never seen since.

Before I became blind, about the only person I encountered who had lost their sight was old Les Hake.

He was a piano tuner. He was blind as a bat, and he used to poke along with a cane. He was a thumper. He'd thump that cane along and if he felt like something was in front of him, he'd wave that cane back and forth and damn near knock you down if you were in the way. He walked with his head like he was looking into the sky.

I tend to walk with my head down. It's just a dumb habit, like playing with my ring. I'm a fumbler.

It must have been a short time after I lost my sight that I was back with Grandma. She had a dark, dingy little, apartment in the back end of a house on North Broad Street, across from the Union School. It only had a couple of windows in it, low ceilings and Linoleum on the floor. She shared the bathroom with the Johns family, who owned the house. He was an old time Lutheran preacher, retired.

Grandma didn't even have a decent chair to sit in. She had the little cot she dragged with her everywhere we moved, set up in the main room. That room served as the kitchen, living room, and dining room. The cot was her bed. She had a studio couch I slept on, in another little room. There were a couple kitchen chairs, a little folding table and a two-burner gas plate. No refrigeration. We had very, very little cupboard space. Uffda!

She never had it real good. She didn't have much, but she could always find a spot for me. Good old Grandma. It was tough going, boy. It almost makes me want to weep, just thinking about it.

When I came back from the Cities, I was newly blinded. I was *really* blind. I couldn't do anything. I spent the day sitting on Grandma's cot. I was like a lump on a log. It was terrible, really.

I remember that Inez and Lois Wilson used to come and get me and we'd go down and hoist a few. Lois was in my class in school, graduating in 1933. She was a little younger than I am. I've kept in touch with her over the years. They seemed to appreciate my predicament, and always have. People shy away from blind people for some reason. They're never comfortable with somebody that can't see. At least I've found it that way, and other blind people have told me that too. Probably sometimes I don't make it easy for them.

Grandma wanted me to get to doing something. She said, "You should learn to type so you could write a letter." I said I thought it was a waste of time, but she went to the library and got a book of instructions on typing, and read it to me.

She still had a little old portable Underwood typewriter she'd had when I came to live with them in 1926. On occasion, she'd type out a letter, I suppose to Aunt Daisy, with one finger. Bing. Bing. Bing.

She put my hands on the home position and I started out with the exercises, where you repeat over, and over, and over, f-g-h-j, f-g-h-j, and I did that on through the book of instructions. My memory was good in those days. I don't know how long it took, but I know I was able to learn the keyboard in one day and use it to type a letter. I'm pretty sure I wrote to Daisy because I felt she would accept the letter with mistakes.

I learned the keyboard that quick. After that, I used it all the time. I really did quite a lot of letter writing. It was a nice way to communicate in those days. In fact, I used it until the last couple of years when my fingers got so crippled up I couldn't reach the keys. I was always grateful to Grandma for starting me on the typewriter, and for giving me the Underwood. That's what I used when I wrote to Lydia later, when she was in St. James.

I was always able to type without error too. I didn't make many mistakes. I never was a speed demon on it but I'll bet we could take those letters I wrote to Lydia out of the box, and I'll bet we would find very few errors, if any!

I'm sure that typewriter must be close to 100 years old. The roller was pretty badly beat by the time I retired it.

LEARNING TO BE BLIND

———

I went to the summer session for the adult blind at the School For The Blind in Faribault, Minnesota, in the summer of '38. Somebody maneuvered me over there for that. There were 10 or 15 old bucks and old ladies there at that time, some of them several years older than me. Some were newly blinded and some had partial vision. They all were struggling really.

A bunch of us would wander downtown and hoist a couple, and stagger back up across the bridge to the school. The blind leading the blind. Quite a procession! I remember there was a guy in that motley group that got goofy drunk and wanted to jump off the bridge into the river or some dumb thing. He was pretty well oiled up. I don't think it took too much to make him that way either. We didn't drink that much. We didn't have any money! It seems to me that we had to restrain him. We did have fun though.

I spent the school year of 1938 and 1939 at the School For The Blind, too. Somehow I got to go back as a special student, because I was older than the high school kids. I was 24, but apparently they felt I was youthful enough to mix with them, and I did. I was comfortable with them, and they with me. I kind of enjoyed the year there.

They had four to a room when I was there. I was in a room with Donald Dedon and Lawrence Elias, and there was a black kid. I never knew he was black for the first month or two I was there!

Both Dedon and Elias had absolute pitch. If somebody would let a fart, they'd tune in on it. They'd hum the note and say what key it was in and then they'd go down and check it on the piano.

Music was big time there. All those kids could play something, and some of them were really, really good. That was the time of the big bands when music was music and you could understand the words. There was lots of jazz. That was in vogue at that time. They really could pump it out too.

They had a five-piece orchestra when I was there, with Donald Dedon, Lawrence Elias, Jacob Neilson, Tim Jergenson, and Don Hunder. Jacob played the drums. They were all blind! I'm sure that at least four of them played piano. I'd say really pretty good piano. Elias was the best one in my book. Other instruments were trumpet, saxophone, and trombone. I thought it was a real good orchestra. They were all good musicians; really gifted! They played anything. You'd hum a tune for them of any kind, and they could play it off like nothing. I really, really enjoyed that part of it.

I started piano tuning then, and took piano lessons for a while. I somehow never did pick up on it. It made me have a better ear for sound, though.

They taught dancing and had dances every week. Some of those girls could really dance too! There was an albino girl I remember dancing with, with my two left feet. She was a true albino. I guess she had the pink eyes, the white, white hair and the white skin. She was about five-foot-ten. It seems to me, I got along pretty good with her. I don't remember dancing with anybody else. She must have impressed me. There were several kids there that were partially bad sighted because of being albino.

I learned rug weaving, basket weaving, chair caning, broom making, a little Braille, wood working, and net tying, all of those crafts that blind people supposedly can do. A bunch of us made a hammock tying net. It was a nice big one too. I don't know who got that. I suppose all they had to do was pay for the cord.

A favorite pastime for some of those kids was if you wanted to have them guide you someplace they'd walk you into a tree. On purpose! And laugh! They'd have a big time.

I would say I had fun there. I had a lot of interesting experiences with the kids.

I finished that school session in 1939 and went back to Mankato to Grandma's.

While I was at the School For The Blind, I learned that state aid for the blind was available. I applied and was accepted and got that. It was meager amounts of money. It seems to me I only got 30 or 35 bucks a month. At that time, though, it was enough to pay for board and room so after I got that, I moved out away from Grandma and did board and room at the Blake's.

They lived downtown across from the Armory on North 2nd Street. Mrs. Blake's husband had taken off into the wilds and she didn't know where he was. She ran a boarding house to support herself and her five kids. Norma was in my class in school. Then there was Chet, Gordy, Delpha, and Junior.

I was more or less introduced to the Seeing Eye, because the woodworking instructor at the School For The Blind, Isaac Thompson, had a German shepherd Seeing Eye guide dog, named Nafty. He could go any place! He just took off like a goosed goose. He was like I am. He had much determination. He was a really great guy.

I don't remember it at all, but I apparently applied to the Seeing Eye, in Morristown, New Jersey and they accepted me. I guess I flew out there. I honestly don't remember. I wonder if they didn't even pay my way out. Somebody must have. It's just a blank spot in my life, I guess. I think I was kind of in a state of shock over having lost my sight.

The Seeing Eye wasn't all that old then. The original people were still there. Morris Frank was the one that got the first Seeing Eye dog, Buddy, and learned to use it. Mrs. Eustis was a wealthy person who actually put up the money to start the Seeing Eye. Humphries was the head instructor. He had gone to Germany where they were already using guide dogs, learned how to use them, and came back. He, among other people, set up the Seeing Eye. He was Mr. Big out there. Debata was kind of the head honcho in the office, and Hutchinson; Elizabeth, I think was her first name, was the secretary and my main contact. Dickerman was my instructor. In fact, I had him for both the dogs I had over the course of my life, Art and Milo.

Art was first. I remember training at the Seeing Eye was really, really good. Quite an experience!

I went out there and got Art in 1940. I was there for four weeks. During that time, I trained with Art and Dickerman on how to use the dogs. You learn how to use a guide dog with the instructor.

We covered the town in many, many different ways and conditions. They put you through the paces, you know? You'd go out every morning and every afternoon for a couple hours each time. When we weren't out practicing, they'd teach you how to care for a dog, currying, cleaning and brushing and all that kind of stuff.

Then we'd go on these trips. They had routes made up where you would encounter everything. They had puddles, and limbs, trees hanging over the sidewalk; holes, bars, wires, and you name it. You worked obstacles of all kinds, moving and stationary, and all kinds of streets and traffic to get the experience so you wouldn't encounter anything new after you left the school. Gradually, starting with no traffic, you'd work up to heavy traffic. A lot of times they'd have you take a cane along, so we learned how to use that.

You had to have an idea where you were headed. Basically all you did was give the dog the command to go forward. If they hit a down curb they'd stop, and you'd put your foot on it and feel so you'd know what it was. If you wanted to go to the right you'd give them a command of, "right" and they'd wheel around and do it.

If there were a low hanging branch or something in the way, they'd stop. There's a technique of sweeping your hand up to touch the limb. That happened often. They'd walk you right up to the limb, and you'd just sweep up, feel of it, and you'd give them a command. If the street was on your right, you'd give them a command to go right and then when they turned to the right, you'd tell them, "left, left, left, left, left", so that after you cleared the limb, you'd get back on the sidewalk again.

We did the training in Morristown. I was in a class of six or eight from all over the country. The only one I really remember was an old guy by the name of Crawford that was from Louisville, Kentucky. He owned an undertaking establishment there. His dog's name was Sister.

The dogs all had names when we got them. Mine were Art and Milo. Both super, super dogs!

One time I came back to the Seeing Eye from one of the trips into town. They had steps going into the building. You'd go up them, through the door and across a lobby to the stairs that went up to the bedrooms. I walked across the lobby and came up to the steps.

When you come to a step, the dogs are trained to stop. You have a technique of foot feeling or hand feeling. When you're ready, you put your foot on the step and give the dog a command to go forward, and they do. I gave old Art the command to go forward, and he did. He went up about four or five steps and then he turned around in his harness to go back down again because Dickerman, the trainer and instructor, was standing at the bottom of the stairs, and he liked Dickerman better than he did me. I bellered a sharp command, "phooey", a verbal correction, and yanked him around. I'm sure I yelled it real loud and tried to straighten him out to go up the steps, but I had a heck of a time with him.

Way back yonder I heard a voice say, "Reward your dog, Sir. Reward your dog!"

I said, "What the hell should I reward him for? He isn't doin' nothin'. He won't go up the stairs."

Humphries, the big time honcho, came cruising down the hall and came up the steps. He snatched the leash out of my hand and said, "Where did you come from?"

I said, "We were downtown."

He said, "Did you cross the street?"

I said "Yeah".

"Safely?"

"Yeah."

He went through the whole rigmarole of stuff that Art had done, and of course Art had done all of the good things, leading me safely through traffic and over hill and dale.

I said, "Yes Sir, yes Sir, yes Sir."

He said, "You don't deserve a dog!" He took Art down the steps and you can imagine how I felt, standing there with my bare face hanging out. I could have died on the spot!

It wasn't too long, and he came back up. He said, "You have to reward your dog. ALWAYS! Carry on."

He was real sharp, so I'm sure I carried on. I felt like crawling into the far corner of my room and hiding, but I gave Art the command to go forward and I guess he went up there this time.

He was really rough, old Humphries. That was one of those times I stuck my foot in my mouth. I've done that many times in my life. I've regretted a lot of them too, but I guess that's me.

I had a real successful training session with Art at the Seeing Eye and I guess I flew back to Mankato with him. They allowed the dogs in the plane at that time, I guess, by special legislation or permission or something.

They never were a trouble in traveling at all. You put them down between your legs. They'd sit down or lie down very quietly. It was easy, and I did some traveling independently too, without anybody helping me.

I don't remember how much time elapsed between Art dying and my going out to get Milo. It couldn't have been very long. I had the same trainer, Dickerman, a coincidence that isn't normal, I'm sure. The training period with Milo was four weeks also, but it seemed like a much shorter time than with Art, because I had done it before and knew the ropes.

I used Art harder than Milo, but the circumstances were different. We lived where I could use him successfully. I used to walk a mile or mile and a half, to and from work, with the greatest of ease.

I was married and had a family and a home when I got Milo. The company I worked for had moved way over to North Mankato, where using Milo to walk to work wasn't practical. Instead, I rode with a fellow, and Milo rode with me. I did use him at work, but not in the same way I used Art. I used Milo mostly in the shop.

Those dogs were unreal. They'd take you through little spaces. If there were room to go, they'd take you through. In the shop, you had people sitting back to back, and there wasn't much room to go down in between, but they'd navigate it. If there was stuff in the way, they wouldn't go!

They were fun. Always ready to go. You'd shake the harness and hold it down there and they'd walk into it. Those dogs helped me live a normal life.

I honestly never encountered anything new, that they hadn't covered at the Seeing Eye in the 25 years I had those dogs. It just was unreal. I was lucky. It was the same thing when I went to the School for the Blind, a real necessary thing in my life. I learned how to be blind.

ART, MY FIRST SEEING EYE DOG,
AND ME. I MUST HAVE JUST GOT HIM
WHEN THIS WAS TAKEN. HE, WE, LOOK
PRETTY YOUNG, C. 1940

LIFE BEGINS

When I came back home and went back to living at the Blakes', I just cruised. I felt like I was turned loose! I got back a little of my independence. I could go any place with Art; fast, and with the greatest of ease, and we did too.

I bought an old junker car while I was there, and taught the Blakes' son, Gordy, how to drive by describing to him what he needed to do! I had him haul me around to my piano tuning jobs. I suppose he was around 14 or 15, maybe 16. I wasn't very successful at tuning pianos, but I did make a few nickels.

One time during the dead of winter there was a howling blizzard brewing, and I decided to go see Grandma. She lived about three or four blocks from the Blakes'. The storm was really terrible. Anybody in their right mind would have never left the house, but old Art and I took off for Grandma's. Going over, it was snowin' and blowin' to beat the devil. You could hardly see your hand in front of your face. I got over there and she opened the door. She was really shocked to see me! She said, "What are you doing here? What are you doing here? You go right back home! Don't you know there's a blizzard?"

So old Art and I turned around and headed for home. I can remember that there were drifts all the way along, and he couldn't walk over them, so he'd jump over them. He was harnessed and I had hold of the harness. He was jumping over those damn drifts and leading me along. Without him I'd have never got back to the Blakes' safely.

Wes and Jess Cornish were both in the CCC camp with me. They've been good friends over all these years. Wes was only in the camp for about three or four months and he went AWOL and dashed home, because he was afraid that his girl, Irene, was going to get away from him.

I sure had fun with them. When I first lost my sight, they would come in and pick me up, and take me out to their farm. Irene would kick the kids out of their bed and give it to me.

I did everything with them. Wes, Jess and I would go hunting pheasants for a meal. Wes would drive and they each had a twenty-two rifle laid across their laps. If they saw a pheasant to the right, Wes would stick his gun out on the right and shoot it. If they saw a pheasant on the left, Jess would shoot out of the left window. They'd go along and as soon as they had enough for supper they'd dash back to the farm, skin 'em out, and cook 'em. They were scrumptious, and it was all just really, really fun.

They took me on fishing trips up north too. I don't remember the lake we went to, but I remember one occasion that Jess had to "go" pretty urgently and he made little "submarines" off the end of the boat. Then to make matters worse, he used an envelope and made a sailboat out of one of them!

Lydia, Irene and Wes were all the same age. I was their junior by a year. Lydia's birthday was in February; I think Wes's in March and Irene's in April.

Before too long, Mrs. Blake decided to hang up the towel on running a boarding house, so I had to find another place to live.

ROMANCE!

I went to live with the Lunzs. Jack Lunz was a little guy. They called him "Little Jack." His mother was Lydia's Aunt Annie, so he was a cousin of Lydia's. He and his wife; mostly his wife - ran a boarding house. Aunt Annie liked me, and she liked Art too.

During the time I was there, I got sicker than a dog, and I had to go to the hospital. I was there for a time, and Aunt Annie took care of Art. I had a bedroom upstairs. There were a couple of landings getting up there. They always talked about Aunt Annie, who was kind of a slight, frail old lady, coming in the house with Art on a leash. She'd throw a half-hitch around the bottom post of the stair railing so she could hold him back, because every time he hit those bottom steps he was off and running, and he would damn near haul her upstairs.

At that time Lydia was teaching at the Mankato Beauty School. She had a room about 8 or 10 blocks from the Lunzs', but came there for her meals. One day, Aunt Annie told Lydia, "You just missed it. There is a guy here that you absolutely have to meet!"

Of course, that guy was me.

When I did meet Lydia, it must have been love at first sight. It was unreal. I didn't have any money. I didn't have nothin'! And dumb? I didn't know two and two! I didn't know why she would ever take on somebody that couldn't see. My first attraction to her must have been her voice and her manner, because I never saw her.

During the time I was romancing her, she decided to close her beauty shop in St. James. She had hired a girl to run it, but it wasn't very successful, so she went back to sell it or close it. I wrote to her every day while she was gone. My letters weren't *real* gooey, but I sure expressed my true feelings for her. She had to know I really loved her and missed her. That was in 1942.

Missing her now is quite different from how I missed her then. Then I knew I would be able to see her again.

It must have been when we were first going together that Lydia and her mother came back to Mankato for a visit. Lydia had her folks' car. She picked me up and we went to the town south of Owatonna to see Lydia's oldest sister, Rose Blaha, and her family. I think that was pretty much the first time I met Grandma too, Lydia's mother. We sat three abreast in the car. I really got along good with Grandma.

When Lydia, Rose and I went out someplace, Rose's husband, Bill asked, "Who is that guy? Is he a relative?" Grandma said, "No, but I think he's gonna be." I always got a kick out of that story.

I was working at Automatic Electric making 35 cents an hour when Lydia was in St. James.

I loved Lydia so much I could hardly stand to be away from her. When I got through work every Friday night, and the buzzer rang, old Art and I hit the trail. We hustled to the bus depot, I'd buy me a ticket and we'd sail right to St. James on the bus. When I'd hop off the bus, she'd be there, waiting for me. I can just see her there. It was super. Boy, that was a happy time. I guess that was the happiest time in my life. Just to be with her. I loved her so much.

My life really began with Lydia. Everything changed completely when I met her. I had lived in a bunch of rotten luck up until then. I had lost my folks and lost my sight, but after I met her, everything changed.

I wrote to her every day and I sailed to St. James on the bus every weekend. I don't remember how long that went on. I don't know if people got tired of me or not. I didn't give them much choice. I was just there. Period!

All of Lydia's family, the Sandmeyers, were just super to me. They treated me so royally it was unreal. You know, somebody that couldn't see, coming into a family like that, you'd think they'd kind of wonder. I would often comment to Lydia how good the whole family was to me, and she'd say, "Why shouldn't they be?" The fact that I couldn't see never entered into my relationship with Lydia or the whole clan. I did appreciate it. That's for sure.

Grandma's full name was Martha Henrietta Brocklesberg Sandmeyer, and Grandpa's name was Joseph Martin Sandmeyer.

I always enjoyed Grandma, and I know she really enjoyed me being around. I went out and did dishes with her or untied her apron or something, just to mess around.

I always sat and visited with Grandpa. He was a big time hunter and trapper, an outdoors guy. He was younger than I am now, but he had the stories that old bucks have, you know. He could go on forever. Lydia took me around to meet all the family during the times I visited.

I don't remember how long Lydia stayed in St. James, but eventually, she came back to Mankato. I like to think she came back to be near me. We couldn't afford to do anything, so our favorite pastime was smooching! We spent a lot of time hugging and kissing. That didn't cost anything.

Art and I chased her for two years and we finally did get married.

LYDIA BY ONE OF THE GARDEN POOLS ON THE
SANDMEYER FARM NEAR ST. JAMES, MN. GRANDMA
SANDMEYER HAD BEAUTIFUL FLOWERBEDS THERE, C. 1938

LYDIA'S FOLKS, JOSEPH MARTIN
SANDMEYER & MARTHA HENRIETTA
BROCKLESBERG SANDMEYER AT CLARA
& RAY HURLEY'S IN ST. JAMES, MN, 1955.

LYDIA'S YOUTH

———

Lydia was born Lydia Georgine Sandmeyer, in St. James, Minnesota, February 22, 1913. I would guess she was born out on the farm. I don't think they bothered with a hospital in those days.

I can't just remember how it happened, but one time Lydia ran a pitchfork into her foot. She was kind of gimping around on it, but out on the farm, you didn't stop for nothin'. You had chores to do and you did them. She was taking a team to the watering tank and hobbling along and jammed a wooded match into her other foot.

Even then, I think they expected her to do her chores, but they didn't get all the match out and she developed a real bad infection in that foot. Grandpa and Grandma wouldn't call the doctor, but finally, I think Flarie, her oldest sister, did. He came out and she had blood poisoning by that time. He lanced it right there and drained it. It was a terrible mess but she recovered from that and many other big time problems in her life.

Another time, they were all at the table eating. Grandma always had Grandma's tea, milk and sugar and boiling water. Lydia got up to get the teakettle to pour Grandma her Grandma's tea. After pouring the cupful she turned back to set the teakettle on the stove, but she set it on the edge and it fell off and scalded her leg from above the knee to the ankle. She had old-fashioned stockings on and she went into the washroom and took them off. Nobody even came in to see if she was okay! She never forgot that.

Grandma would say, "Oh, you and your doctors. You and your doctors!" But that's the way they thought in those days.

Lydia and her brother Walter got along really well. There was a sister,

Ida, between them, but when he did anything he always wanted Lydia to go along.

Grandpa and the boys did a lot of trapping for furs. They'd skin them out, put them on slats or boards, stretch them inside out, and then sell them. They ran big trap lines, and trapped muskrat, and mink, weasel, coon, fox, wolves, skunk, and anything and everything. Even in the old days, furs were worth quite a bit of money per hide.

Walter had a trap line run for muskrat. It was snowing one day and he talked Lydia, who was in her early teens then, into going with him.

MY BEAUTIFUL WIFE, LYDIA SANDMEYER, A GRADUATE OF THE PARISIAN SCHOOL OF BEAUTY CULTURE. SHE OWNED AND OPERATED BEAUTY SHOPS FROM 1931-1942 AND WAS AN INSTRUCTOR AT THE MANKATO SCHOOL OF BEAUTY CULTURE FROM 1942-1943, C. 1940

They checked the trap line, and were a goodly hunk away from home when the wind started to blow. They picked up and turned, and walked into a full-blown blizzard.

It blew snow just really, really bad. You get in that kind of stuff and it's like being blind! You can get lost in a three-foot circle! Anyhow, they plodded along and he was dragging Lydia behind. She just wanted to sit down and rest, but he knew if she did he'd never be able to get her up again, so he made her stay up on her feet.

They finally ran into a fence. He didn't really recognize it, but they guessed at the direction to go in, and followed the fence. All the time she wanted to sit down or lay down. She was really pooped, but he never let her rest.

He practically carried her, I'm sure, and they finally got to where they could see the barn. She always said she was sure, if he had let her rest, she would have died out there. They would have never been able to find her.

One of the boys, either Leo or Walter, trapped a young gray wolf. They brought him back to the farm, made a pen and kept him in it. They had him on a chain inside and he could just about reach the fence he was penned up in.

Lydia said he always hated Walter; just didn't like him. Maybe Walter was the one who trapped him. I don't know.

Lydia named the wolf Tippi and eventually tamed him so she could play with him. She'd throw a rag, or a stick, or anything, and Tippi would fetch it back to her and lay it at her feet. Then she'd pick it up and throw it again. He would do that for a long time.

One time she threw something and turned to go. He grabbed her in the hind end and dragged her back into the middle of the pen. He wanted to play some more. I guess he sunk his old fangs in her real good. So, she threw something again and he watched her real close while he went to fetch it. She eventually got him far enough away, so she could dash out of the pen and he couldn't reach her. She never went back to play with him after that.

Another time, Leo and Walter were repairing the fence on the pen. They were digging a hole to put in a new post. Old Tippi ambled up and sunk his teeth into the calf of Walter's leg. He had a boot on but Tippi put those big fangs through the boot and everything else. Walter flipped him over and told Leo to go get a tool. Well, Tippi lost his big fangs that day. He wouldn't sink them into a boot again.

They said when they got ready to sell his hide, they skinned him and put him on the slat, hung him up, and he reached from the tip of the nose to the tip of the tail, eight feet. He was a big one!

Two of Lydia's sisters, Clara and Valeria (Flarie), the Sandmeyer twins, married brothers, Ray and Sylvester (Vet) Hurley. Their brother, Dan Hurley, who had been living in Seattle, Washington, was pursuing Lydia. The brothers all wanted to marry Sandmeyers!

LYDIA SANDMEYER AND
'HAPPY' THE FOX, C. 1925

THE BETROTHAL

I was really lucky to latch on to Lydia. I honestly don't remember how I proposed to her. Isn't that dumb? It must have been pretty simple because I *still* didn't have any money.

I bought her a diamond wedding ring. I don't know how I scraped enough together for that, but I did. I had a friend, Ed Huntinger, who ran the jewelry store, and I know he gave me a good deal on that diamond. He didn't give it to me. That's for sure. But I know it was a good deal.

Lydia lost that diamond a couple of times. Once the set came off and she lost it at work. People dropped down, and scraped and scratched through all kinds of junk and eventually came up with it. Mary has the diamond in a locket now. Lydia wanted her to have it.

I'm not sure how long we were engaged, but I would guess it was less than a year. We would have gotten married on my birthday, but as I always said, I moved the wedding up a week because I was half afraid she was going to get away from me! Hurley, the guy from Seattle, was after her too. Happily, I beat his time.

Lydia would say, "Ah, you and your BS."

Lydia had a lot of guts, taking on somebody that couldn't see and only making 35 cents an hour. Uffda! She must have been out of her mind! But it all went along real well. She never looked on me as one that couldn't see. She expected me to do everything, and I would say I didn't disappoint her. I was able to do everything within reason.

We were married June 12, 1943 in St. James, at the Catholic Church. It was a very simple wedding. Lydia and I marched down the aisle together to the altar. She wore her $11 wedding dress and I had a suit.

The bridesmaid was Lydia's niece, Caroline Hurley Dougherty, and the groomsman was my cousin, Fred Lamp.

After the ceremony, we went out to Lydia's mother and dad's farm and had a scrumptious fried chicken dinner. I can *still* taste that chicken. It was just super! I'm sure I made a pig out of myself, 'cause my manners were kind of rough and I was hungry.

While we were out there, all the kids did a chivaree. There were lots of kids too. I didn't know anything about a chivaree or what you were supposed to do. I guess after they made so much noise outside, with pounding on discs and cowbells and pans and all that, we finally went out on the porch. You're supposed to smooch while you're there. They'd all yell and holler and carry on, and then the groom is supposed to pay off. In the old days, older people used to do the chivaree and the groom would give them money so they could go buy booze or beer – but not for the kids. Anyhow, I didn't have any money, so we got by with just smooching.

It was terrible really, to be so broke, but we were so in love we didn't give a crap if we had anything or not.

We went on a honeymoon. I wonder where that money came from. Maybe Lydia paid for that!

We had a reservation to go fishing on Farm Island Lake up north. It must have been close to Lake Mille Lacs or someplace up there. We'd bought a car from my uncle, a Chevrolet coupe. Lydia hated the thing and didn't trust it.

We had rented a house from Vernon Tufftie, at 627 Blue Earth Street in West Mankato, not too far from where I live now. He was in school the same time I was, but not in my class, as I remember.

We drove the car there and left it at the house, and we took the bus up to the lake. We had the resort owner come in and pick us up, and Lydia, Art and I spent the week up there in a very nice cabin.

We had a real, real nice honeymoon. The fishing license for the two of us was $1.50. We came back with eight Northern and two Walleye. It was a fun time.

I don't know how far it was to work from the house on Blue Earth Street, maybe 15-20 blocks, but I walked there with Art, every day, with the greatest of ease.

After a few months, Vernon wanted to do some remodeling, so he asked us to move. Then we rented another place up beyond the Lincoln School on Shaubut Street. Lydia absolutely hated that place from day one. It was so old and cruddy. The old lady that owned it had all kinds of stuff in it.

We weren't in that house very long and we moved, in the winter, to an upstairs apartment downtown on Hickory Street, real close to St. John's Church and the Episcopalian church, and about a block from the courthouse. Everything was handy, and it wasn't too far from Automatic Electric either, about 10 or 12 blocks.

OUR WEDDING PHOTO TAKEN
IN ST. JAMES, MN, JUNE 12, 1943.

ME, MARY, ART AND GRANDMA FOOTNER, 1944.

MAKING A LIFE

I did speaking engagements when I first came back from the Seeing Eye. I spoke mostly at high schools and farm bureaus.

Of course I talked about the Seeing Eye, the training and how to take care of your dog. I always demonstrated. I used to have fun. I would get into an auditorium and do the balcony and the aisles and whistle around, and up into the stage door and out on the stage. I always had Art walk right to the edge of the stage. Quick, you know... and of course he'd stop right at the edge. They'd swear to God I was going to go off for sure! I would take questions from the audience. They really ate it up!

One time, one of Flarie Hurley's kids, Neil, came to visit us. I don't know why, but I got a wild hair and told Lydia that we were going to be gone awhile and I took Neil out and had him back the Chevrolet sedan out of the garage. He'd never driven a lick. Setting in the car, in the garage, I told him what to do over and over. I made him repeat what I'd told him, and he finally felt that he knew, so I had him back the car out of the garage and we took off.

We drove on a road (kind of a cow path) down where West High School is now (There was a slough down in there then.) and then turned up on Pleasant to come out to where my house is now. My Uncle Pete and Aunt Maude lived down there, so I was really familiar with the area. Well, I was familiar with the whole town then. I could tell you exactly where everything was! Anyhow, it was wintertime, and he had to buck snow through that road.

Lydia just raved when I got back home. "Stupid, stupid. Taking a kid that's never driven, out on an icy day. "You haven't got good sense!"

I could give you Neil's number in Kissimmee, Florida and you could call him, honest to God, and ask him who taught him to drive, and he'd tell you, "Harry Footner, and he's blind!"

That was the second kid I taught to drive in the same way. The first was Gordy Blake, who now lives in Austin, Texas. I had them go over and over what they were supposed to do and then they took off.

There are damn few things I haven't done, really. I've had some weird experiences, and done some strange things. I always said I couldn't drive a car after I was blind, but actually, I did that too!

One time I was with a bunch of guys and I said, "I sure wish I could drive." It was in the wintertime, so they headed for Lake Crystal. I remember I finally asked them where we were and they said, "We're on Lake Crystal. Now you slide over here and drive." That's exactly what I did. They told me "left" and "right" and I drove all over that lake on the ice and snow!

When Lydia and I were first married, we headed out every weekend. I remember one time we went by the farm where I worked that summer as a kid, the year my parents died.

Mostly we went out to have fun, hunting, fishing, and traveling. We used to go to her brother Walter and Evelyn's place quite often. The pheasant hunting was really good down there at that time. They'd stick me in a cornrow and I'd play dog. I'd march along and chase the birds up for them to shoot. I did that with the Cornish boys, the guys I was with in the CCC camp, even before Lydia and I were married.

Fall is my favorite season, when the weather cools down a little bit and the hunting and fishing seasons come along. Lydia, Walter, and I would go out at the crack of dawn and sit in the duck blind when it was cold, windy, and rainy, and we'd hunt ducks. Lydia was an excellent shot. She hunted from the time she was a little kid and we sure didn't stop hunting after we got married. She could scrape the sky with that old 12-gauge!

One time, two ducks got up and Walter told Lydia to take them. They were really high, but she knocked them both down. There were a couple of guys across the slough from where we were. One of them yelled,

"Jesus Christ! Did you see that? It was a god-damned woman shooting!" They were shocked to see a woman shoot like that.

My Uncle Pete hunted from the time he was a little kid too, but he never had a car, so any hunting he did, he walked to. He was good at walking. He worked for a gravel company and walked two or three miles to work every day, rain or shine, winter or summer. He ran a steam shovel, dragging sand and gravel out of the river.

In those days you could walk down the street and do a left, walk along the railroad tracks and out into the country. There were pheasants, and rabbits, and what-have-you, within walking distance.

Uncle Pete had a series of good hunting dogs, all named, "Smoky." I don't know how many Smoky(s) we went through over the years! They were always really, really good hunters. One of the later Smoky(s) was so excited when she saw Uncle Pete's gun come out, she wagged her tail so furiously, and beat it so hard against things, it actually burst open.

Uncle Pete loved Lydia. That's for sure. He didn't even swear around her, and I'm sure that was about the end of the line, boy! Lydia saw the good in him and she thought we should take him hunting.

We took him duck hunting and pheasant hunting. He was a fairly good shot too. I remember hunting ducks out on Eagle Lake, sitting on a muskrat pile with Lydia. He was down on another one, and they were shooting ducks. They'd drop them in the water and Smoky would go get them. She was a really, really good pheasant dog too.

Uncle Pete had a double barrel 12-gauge shotgun with the hammers on the outside. They always said, and I guess he did too, that it had a hair trigger, that if you'd just barely touch the triggers, they'd go off.

One time when we were hunting, he dropped that gun and it went off. We were all standing around there, you know. It didn't hit anybody, but that ended Uncle Pete's hunting with us. Lydia was afraid of that gun. It went off too easy.

Pretty early on, I bought Lydia a Browning automatic. That was big time in those early days! She did love to hunt.

I loved to dance. Lydia and I danced some, but it was the same old thing. We didn't have money enough to stretch to that kind of stuff. I'm not very good at any of them, but I suppose the main dance we did was the foxtrot. I still would love to be able to really waltz.

I love all kinds of music, especially the big bands and that kind of music. There are so many songs that remind me of Lydia, like, *I'll Be Seeing You*, and *Always*. It gets me.

We had television right away, as soon as it was available. I don't remember the year. We had it, but I never was much interested in it.

Lydia and I were real, real close to my Grandma. We had everyday contact, took things to her, and did things for her every day. She loved Lydia. Everybody loved Lydia! Grandma died May 16, 1947 in Blue Earth County.

We must have lived in the apartment on Hickory Street about three years. During that time, Mary was born.

Mrs. Edney, who owned the house we were living in, didn't like the idea of a kid and a dog over her head, and I think Lydia must have been pregnant with Joel. I suppose the prospect of having another kid upstairs didn't appeal to her, so she told us we should look for something else, and we did.

We have two kids, Mary Martha Footner and Joel Harry Footner. Mary was born July 9, and Joel was born November 20. I left the naming of the kids to Lydia. I'm sure I pushed for Joel to be named Richard, to keep with the family tradition that every other oldest male was a Harry or a Richard alternately, but I had a small part in the program.

When Mrs. Edney asked us to move, we bought the place where I live now. When we moved here, there was a pasture across the street with cows in it. It's hard to believe when you look there now, with a house on every lot. Joel was born after we moved here. I love the house and the area and everything about it. We lived out half of our lives in this house!

Mary was three years old when we moved here. A neighbor, Mrs. Mork, was getting to be quite old then. She loved Mary, and she asked her what her name was. Mary told her, "My name is Mary Martha Footner and I'm three years old."

ART AND ME ON THE WAY TO WORK AT
AUTOMATIC ELECTRIC MANUFACTURING
COMPANY, 1946.

'ON THE LINE' AT THE AUTOMATIC WITH ART BY
MY SIDE, C. 1942

AUTOMATIC ELECTRIC

I graduated from high school with Bill Klammer. He was bent on me getting a job. He tried to set me up in a broom factory, and I tried piano tuning, but nothing seemed to go very good.

Finally, in 1942, he said, "You should come to work at Automatic Electric," which I did. They sat me down on a production line and I built relays. I didn't have any trouble at all doing it. I could do almost anything the girls could do. I couldn't see to adjust them. That required sight, but anything that didn't absolutely require sight, I was able to do.

It wasn't too long and they put me in charge of the line, and awhile longer and they made me a foreman. I don't remember how long I'd worked on the production line when they made me a supervisor. I was on that job for a time. I supervised probably 40, 50 or 60 girls and a couple of guys too.

Eventually they brought me into the managing section and I was in that position until I retired.

During the war, Automatic Electric had two satellite plants, one in Madelia and one in Mountain Lake. I supervised both plants and had a production line in the home plant during that time. I had a driver that hauled me hither and yon. It was an interesting time.

We made relays, contributing to the war effort, and the company was given the Army and Navy "E" award, for excellence. They had a ceremony in the Armory.

Of course, they had old Art and I up on stage to receive the award. Big time officials came down to present it. They used me. I'm sure they picked me out of the group because I had Art. Everybody loved Art. I don't remember if I had to respond. I suppose at least with a "thank you." I don't think I made a speech.

I hired all of the people in Madelia and in Mountain Lake. That was really fun. They never forget you. In fact, not long ago I went to St. James and one of the girls I had hired was in the restaurant there. She came to the table and said, "You won't remember me, but you hired me 33 years ago." That was funny.

A short time ago, I went to a gathering of the old employees from the shop. One of the girls there said I sat by her the day I started, and that was in 1942. It seems like I can go downtown or anyplace and run into someone that worked for me 40 or 50 years ago. It just is unreal.

I think, most of the people initially thought I could see. I sat at a desk when they came in. I have fooled people. That's for sure.

I had pretty good hearing in those days and, although I couldn't see, nobody fooled me on anything. I had a second sense or something. I knew what was going on. I could feel it. I still do.

I had fun working. The girls were always really good to me. They worked real hard, so I was successful on the job.

The business changed hands twice during the time I worked for them. It was Automatic Electric when they first started. Then it was bought out by Telex and then bought out again by Mid-tex. Today, it's called Mid-com. A part of it moved to Watertown, South Dakota where they manufacture transformers now. I retired after working for them 37 years. I was 65.

I don't think we ever had any health benefit. I didn't get a pension either. That went into effect a few months after I retired. I got a radio and a fishing rod.

Other than my work for Automatic Electric, I don't think any part of the family was involved in World War II, except that Aunt Daisy's husband, Uncle Eli Lamp did serve in the Army in World War I. He didn't say much about his experiences. It didn't seem like any of the guys that were in the war talked about it.

BLIND NO MORE

After I met Lydia I wasn't blind anymore. I'm blind again now, but with Lydia, I saw every flower, every bird, and every blade of grass. I saw everything. I never thought about it. I don't think she thought about it either. It was just an automatic dialogue with her. We'd go for a drive and she'd say, "Oh, there's a new house being built there." I saw it just as well as she did.

We had lots of fun, and did *everything*. We lived a completely normal life, even though I couldn't see. There was never any talk about me being blind. She never accepted me as a blind person. She expected me to do everything, and I don't think I disappointed her. I always did the things that blind people just don't do. I went hunting and fishing, traveling, *everything*. And we did a *lot* of those *kinds* of things. Nobody can realize what it was like, unless they were here.

Our kids lived a very normal life. In fact, they both say they had more than other kids did. They did more, saw more, and had more.

After the kids came along, Lydia didn't work. She took care of the kids. She did lots of sewing and gardening, and planted flowers. She painted this house, including the screens and storm windows. They weren't combinations, and this is a tall, high house. She talked about standing on the top rung of the ladder and doing the peak. Joel told me how high it was; 36 feet or something like that. It's a long way up, anyhow. She sure could work. She just could do anything.

I don't remember what year it was, but she decided to take up painting. She actually only painted one year, to amount to anything. She did wildlife and watercolors mostly. She did an oil of Jesus that she really, really enjoyed doing and was proud of. People have looked at it and said it was really a good one. I guess her wildlife watercolors are really good too.

When the kids were in school, she took on some jobs. She worked for Donny Bateman, adjusting relays. He was a private contractor, doing work for Automatic Electric. I would send the parts to Donny and he'd build the relays. Lydia would go down and pick them up, bring them to the house here and adjust them. Then she'd take them back down to Donny and he'd deliver them to Automatic Electric.

I graduated from high school with Donny. He was in a real bad motorcycle accident and in a coma for a long time. After he came to, he was paralyzed from under his shoulders, down. He had use of his arms, and the use of his head. He had a house moving company at one time, and he could do anything mechanical.

He always thought he had it better than I did. We kind of joked back and forth about who was better off and we both thought we were better off than the other guy. Both of us did well under the circumstances. I think that was the reason we felt comfortable joking about it.

He was a real nice guy, with a super nice wife, Edith.

Lydia worked for him for two or three years. She was really, really quick. After that job, she went to work for Johnson Reel, building fishing reels. It was the same thing there. She could outwork any and all of them. I don't remember how many years she worked for them, but several. Then she went to work for the Wornson and Polzin Dental Lab. That was a job she really enjoyed. She always wished she could have done a different job there, but I'm sure she did so well on the job they put her on, they wouldn't let her do anything else. She worked for them for quite a few years, until she retired.

DONALD AND EDITH BATEMAN AT
HIS SHOP, C. 1960

WINE MAKING AND CANNING

We always had a garden and had *everything* in it. We had fruit trees that grew and bore well too: apples and plums, raspberries, and chokecherries for jelly and wine. Especially wine!

I would guess within the first 10 years we were married, we started making wine. We made lots of it and it was good stuff!

We did a lot of canning too. When we would do canning or wine-making I helped clean the vegetables and fruit. I always did 99 percent of the lifting and carrying. I didn't let Lydia do anything.

We canned everything, including meats. In fact I have a jar of meat down in the basement that Lydia canned several years ago, that would be as good as the day it was put down there, if it hasn't rusted a hole through the cover.

I always said Lydia was the best cook west of the Mississippi, and that took in a lot of territory. Everything she did was good! I don't know that she had a real favorite thing to make. We always had variety. She was not one to make the same thing over and over. She made new dishes all the time.

She was always trying a new recipe. She said that anybody who can read could be a good cook. Usually, she made the recipe right down the line the first time. If it needed doctoring up, then she did it on the second try. I think that's why all of her cooking was so good. What she did was always 99 and 9/10 percent to perfection. Really!

She made her own blend of seasoning. We still have the recipe and use it all the time. It is a seasoning she made by trial and error until she had it the way she wanted. It took her a long time to develop. It's kind of like Lawry's and those other kinds of seasoning, but it is very distinctive.

It is Lydia's seasoning, period. I have given quite a bit of it away, and all of the people that have it, seem to enjoy it. It's different, that's for sure.

There was a tip she got, I think from an old Chinaman about putting sugar with veggies that kept them fresher longer. She cut things up differently than anybody. People loved her stuff, and loved the way she did it.

For that matter, she folded my underwear differently than anybody. She always got a kick out of me telling her that I honestly did appreciate the nice job she did folding my clothes.

Lydia made good candy too. I'm Norwegian. I love candy. I just love chocolates of any kind.

Lydia and I made wine for many, many years. She didn't have all the fancy stuff like I have now with a hydrometer and a thing that works perfect to measure the wine into the bottle when you're filling it. She could tell by looking at the batch what stage it was in, and what it needed.

We always had a good stock in the wine room.

We made wild plum, and elderberry and rhubarb, and rhubarb and raspberry. We made dandelion wine, and apricot. We had a beautiful apricot tree in the yard, and made several batches from that. For years we always had wine going. Good stuff!

She finally didn't feel like making wine. Over several years I would ask her periodically if we shouldn't make another batch of wine, but she didn't feel up to it, or didn't want to.

I eventually threw all the wine bottles away. I'd say there were at least a couple hundred. I had emptied them, down the hatch you know? One time I asked her again about making a batch of wine. It was some time after she had had a heart attack.

She said, "Oh yah. Let's go ahead. Let's make wine." So we started up again, and we made three or four more batches while she lived.

I made one batch when she was really down in bed, and that was kind of a failure. It was rhubarb, and I didn't squeeze enough of the juice out of the pulp. It was kind of light.

DAY-TO-DAY LIFE

I imagine it was when Mary was in high school we made an ice rink out in the backyard. The big city rink was only about six or seven blocks from our house, but we still made our own rink. I borrowed skates from somebody, and went out and did my thing. Mary and I skated together with no problem except that my ankles were on the ice as much as the skate blades. I should have had those two runner deals that they used to put on the little kids!

Anyhow, I skated around and around with Mary. Then, of course, I thought I could do it alone. I'm sure Mary probably told me not to try, but it was another challenge. You know, there's no way in hell I could have kept my directions on ice like that. It was stupid. But I still did it, and I remember taking a hell of a flop when I ran into the side of the rink where we banked it up.

We all hunted, so Joel had to have a gun. Lydia carved a stock out of a piece of wood and had a little piece of pipe for a barrel. She drilled holes in it and screwed it onto the stock. He hunted from the time he was probably four years old!

Lydia was always good at spotting downed game, and she taught the kids that from little on too. When you shoot something it falls down away from you and you line it up with something so you can find it. Joel is a real expert at that. He did it from little on. One time we came out of the cornfield from hunting pheasants and Lydia asked, "Where's your gun, Joel?" He had laid it down back in the field but he said, "I marked it. I'll find it." He was four or five years old. The weeds were taller than he was, but he wandered in and pretty soon he came out with his gun.

One time, Lydia thought we should have a square dance, so we took the carpeting up and emptied the room. We had a nice hardwood floor in there and the room is fairly good sized. We hired a woman to call the square dance. She brought her music and we invited neighbors. There were about 8 or 10 maybe. I tried one dance, but I had two left feet, so I abandoned that idea. But it really went over real well. They never forgot it. That was big time! In those days we didn't drink, and still had a good time!

We traveled a lot. Mary says she had been in every state west of the Mississippi before she graduated from high school. We always took the kids, little or big. We never left them behind. They went every place we went. Even when Joel was a baby, we went out to the West Coast on a big time trip.

MARY, JOEL AND MILO, MY SECOND
SEEING EYE DOG,
C. 1952

We stayed in motels. We were always headed to see family, but we never stayed with the families out west very long. Two or three days and we were on our way.

Growing up, I would say Joel and Mary enjoyed having Art and Milo around, and could treat them pretty much like family pets. They were different though, you know. They couldn't be fed odd stuff.

Both dogs were about two and a half to three years old when I brought them home, and both of them lived to be about 12 1/2 years old, pretty old for big dogs. I remember taking Art to a vet once, but I never took Milo to a vet. All they needed was food, water, and care. Nowadays people run up bills of thousands of dollars for the dumb dog! You can get dental work for them and the whole bag!

After the kids were gone, we traveled with my sister Daisy and her husband Norton Schmidt. They had a nice big motor home, and the four of us went coast-to-coast, border-to-border. We would go, sometimes for three or four weeks at a time, and never had a hassle. We really got along well.

After we were home, I could tell people more about the trips than they could. I have a good memory and I enjoy traveling. I saw that stuff just as well as they did, the same as today, really. People describe things to me and I get a good mental picture of it. Of course, I have an advantage over people who have *never* seen.

We spent lots of time up North with Nort and Daisy, especially when they were building their house. We helped too. I was a gopher; go for this, and go for that. I did a lot of carrying and hauling and holding. One time, we were doing something with 12-foot long 2X8's. Nort had me hauling them to wherever he was nailing them up. They had a dog, Kippi. Nort was kneeling down along side Kippi, petting her and talking to her, and all that good stuff, and I came along with this 2x8, and I whacked him in the head with the end of that thing! I knocked him ass over teakettle. Oh God was he mad! He really fumed! He eventually cooled off, but he sure was mad. He never swore, but I almost think he might have then.

We had lots of fun doing that place, though. It was a lot of hard work, but it was a lot of fun and we went up often. We were working yet at that time. We used to dash home from work and Lydia would have gotten food prepared, ready to take up.

We had lots of fun with Nort and Daisy. We never had a problem and we were together a lot.

Lydia and I flew out to California to visit my brother Dick and his wife, Doris. At that time, they were flying real high. They had a yacht, a big, big, boat with a poop deck and all that goes, and of course we had a big time Captain's cap and all that good stuff. We were really playing the role!

They lived in Huntington Beach at that time and Dick was the Commodore, or whatever they call them, heading up this group of people that had big time yachts there at the marina. One time when we were down there, Ed Brown, who was the governor of the state at that time, came by. They were on a first name basis and Dick introduced me to him. I, like a dummy, stood by and didn't introduce Lydia to him, and it was kind of a crappy deal. That was one of my failures that stick in my mind. As I remember it, we were glad to get back home.

We flew into Northern Canada on our 38th wedding anniversary to go fishing. We caught great gobs of fish, and it was the same old story. Lydia took my place at the fish-cleaning table. She could clean about two to the other guys' one. She always had her hand in everything big time. If it was work, she could do it.

When we launched the boat, we had to put it through a whole bunch of rocks and I remember helping the other guy that was in the boat, shove off. I actually kind of ran through the rocks. I'd sure have a hell of a time running through rocks today. Holy buckets. I have a hard time walking on flat carpeting.

Lydia loved to share everything. Good times. She had to share her good time with everyone; like traveling or going to the lake. She took Grandpa and Grandma. I remember one time; we took her sister Clara out West. We very seldom went alone. She was sharing our good time with someone else. We took the neighbors on both sides up north fishing. On some occasions, we paid for it all too.

She was always first hand to help somebody that was having a problem. If people were just moving into a new home, she was always there with a hot dish or something to eat for their first meal. With new babies she was there. With people who were dying, she was there.

Mary and Joel had a pony, Patchy, and I remember the first time we brought the pony home. Lydia gave every kid in the neighborhood a ride, almost to the point that Mary didn't get to ride!

At the same time, she didn't deny our family *anything*. The kids had as much as, or more than, other kids in the neighborhood.

There were people who wanted Lydia and I to tell our story but she would never give in to having any kind of publicity. It embarrassed her. She didn't like to have her picture taken or her voice recorded. She was very humble and modest.

Lydia was so conservative and so frugal it was unreal. She was always afraid we wouldn't have enough in our old age to survive. I kept telling her to spend it, but she never did. Everything with her was "good enough," especially for herself. With me she was generous.

She handled the purse strings. Oh, we did it together but the only things she gave me a free hand with, were the cars and the food.

We always had a good, responsible, reliable car and lots of good food. We had big cars too; Lincolns and big Buick's; nice ones, not just junkers. I loved that Lincoln, and I liked the last car we had real well too, a big Buick. We bought those two vehicles and other cars new. We had a big black four-door Buick with a gray interior, in the early days. Uffda! That was something. Plush.

I didn't vote until after Lydia and I were married. We always voted then. No one questioned her honesty in the voting booth, so we voted together, hand in hand. We got the two ballots and she did her thing. I think our politics were pretty close, although sometimes she didn't see my way.

I think both Lydia's parents died of heart attacks. Grandma first. They had moved off the farm and were living in

MARY AND I SKATING ON THE RINK ON OUR BACK YARD, 1962.

St. James. After Grandma died, Grandpa went to live with Lydia's sister, Clara. She took care of him until he died. I don't remember the year, but it was a couple years after Grandma died.

Clara always got stuck with the old people. Her husband Ray died, and she took care of his bedridden mother for years and years and years. Ray's mother was a big, big woman and Clara was real small.

After Lydia and I retired, we walked a lot every day, anywhere from two to five miles. It was a common sight to see us going down the avenue hand in hand. We just loved it. I got close to nature because she described everything as we went along, so I never missed a thing. It was all a part of our being together.

When Lydia was ill, and she wasn't able to walk, I put her in a wheelchair and she'd give me the gee and the haw with a "No, no, no, no!" She made sure I wouldn't dump her into a mud puddle. It worked too.

The last time we did that, we went down the alley and a couple of people came out to greet her. When we got out on Moreland Avenue and Ridge Court, all the way along, the people came out to greet her. Honestly. From all over! I don't know how long it took us to do the route, but quite awhile. Everybody enjoyed her.

After I retired, she never did a washing. She never made a bed. I always got and held her coat. I always opened the door for her. Always. Not just once in awhile. If she went to get her own coat or jacket, I'd chew on her. I said I'd get it. I treated her like the lady she was.

Lydia was different. She loved to be able to work! Much of her life she couldn't, but then she still did, even though most people would have given up.

Her health problems started two weeks after we got married. She had an appendectomy and it seemed like it went on and on and on. We counted major surgeries one time, and I don't remember, but the number was pretty high for both of us. I had gallstones and prostate surgery and I had lots of eye surgeries. Most of the eye surgeries were done before we were married.

I miss being told to put my head up. "Stand straight! You look like a little old man. Like Little Jack!" and I'd remember what Little Jack looked like, so I did stand straighter. She didn't want me to be all bent out of shape like a little old man. I always told her if I straightened up I'd bump my nose instead of the top of my head. I didn't want my nose to be any bigger. All in good fun!

I wore a hat for many years, after we were married. I really like a hat. I wish they'd come back into fashion. I think it really, really dresses you up. You set it on the side a little bit, a little cocky.

I started to get bald young, and I am *really* a baldy now. I wasn't in a barbershop for over 50 years. Lydia always timed my haircuts, so if she had to go to the hospital, she'd be sure to get my hair cut before she went. That's why I say she was different. She was still cutting my hair when it needed it, up until she died.

She had at least three heart attacks, but she'd sit in her chair and have me sit on the floor. She'd reach over with a clipper, scissors, and comb, and she'd whack 'em off! Just like always. I had to spin around on my rear end to be pointed in the right direction for her.

Red rose was Lydia's favorite flower. Early on, when they weren't so expensive, I bought a dozen of them on several occasions during the year. In later years, she still loved them, but she didn't want more than one at a time. "It costs too much!" she would say.

We always had a flower garden, and still do. I was going to tear it out and put in grass, but Mary and Joel thought we should just hang tough and keep it up. The way it is, with the stuff that's in it, it pretty much takes care of itself. Mary adds a little every year. We still have a Seven Sisters rose.

Lydia got a piece of it from her sister Ida, many years ago. It came from a climbing red rose that Lydia's aunt and uncle had. They had it for many, many, many years. Everyone figures that rosebush has proliferated in the family for over 100 years.

Lydia gave many, many plants away. She gave a shoot from the Seven Sisters rose to our grandson, Joseph. I dragged her out in a wheelchair. She had her little shovel, and she found a root that had started from one of the long canes. She whacked it loose from the main cane, dug it, and shook it out, and I think she wrapped it up in wet paper towels, stuck it in a box, addressed it, and sent it to Joseph at LaGrange, Kentucky.

He planted it, and today it has canes that are 25 to 30 feet long along a fence! I guess, this past season, it was just beautiful. Really, really a showy piece.

Lydia always had a way with wild things. She trained a chipmunk to almost turn summersaults. She got him so he finally would come to me and crawl around. I'd stick sunflower seeds in my pocket and he'd come up my leg and crawl into the pocket and crawl out and look at me and go back in. It was crazy. He'd crawl up onto the top of my head. We had a lot of fun that year! I think that was the first year I retired. She had everything trained. The pigeons and chipmunk, and she had a coon until he bit her.

We've had a bird feeder in the back yard for 34 years. It is a wing feeder and is fairly good sized. Where the birds have clamped their toes on the wings, they've actually worn a hole through the board. One piece is broken off. The other is still hanging on, but with a hole through the wood from clamping the toes.

The deck is showing wear too. It used to be smooth cement, but now it's all pocked with holes from the birds pecking seeds up there.

Lydia had a real bad time with osteoporosis. She had collapsed vertebrae in the lumbar region. They had a new procedure going at the Mayo Clinic in Rochester where they injected bone cement and made the vertebrae fast, so you couldn't move them.

They said she was the 13th person in the U.S. to have that done. Now if that's true or not, I don't know. Some of the people that just were so miserable they wished they could die, got up after this procedure and walked away with no pain at all. Zero. It really worked! With Lydia, I think it did help some. So did the pills. I'm sure her case was so bad there wasn't much help they could give her.

She had a physical going into Mayo and she spent 8 or 10 days in the cardiac section with specialists hovering over her day after day. Her heart was so bad. I don't know what the deal was, but they finally said she could have that procedure done, but they did it very carefully. Then after she got out of there, they still told her she'd be lucky to get home. They didn't make any bones about it. But she weathered that storm and we got home, and we went right to the hospital from Rochester.

She was admitted, and I'm sure our doctor, Dr. Putzier, enrolled her in the hospice program, I think mostly because the doctors in Rochester told Lydia that she wouldn't live to get home, that her heart was so bad. The hospice program was really, really good for Lydia and I. They were all just super, super good to us. The nurses and the home care people were very, very nice. Of course being in that program, the cost of it was little or nothing.

The nurses came to the house twice a week and checked her vitals. From their findings, they reported to the doctor, and the doctor prescribed medication.

The house wasn't a house of the dying at all. Never. As long as she lived, I know people enjoyed coming here. She always had stories to tell.

We had the hospital bed about four feet from the bathroom. If she was able to move, I was able to take her to the bathroom. I did everything, really, that a nurse would do, around the clock. I slept in a chair much of the time. If she moved, I was awake and doing my thing. She was fun to take care of, really. She was so appreciative. Nobody ever did anything for her that she didn't express how much she really appreciated it.

The room we lived in is about 18 feet long and about 14 feet wide. It has big sliding glass doors, the eight-foot size. That was something she insisted on too. It really makes the room very nice. I still spend most of my time in that room.

I still feed the birds. People who come mention the birds, and if they don't know what it is, if they can accurately describe it, I can tell them. I was a birder for 58 years! As soon as we had a place, we started feeding birds, even though that was not a real common thing early on.

In fact, I still have the first bird feeder we ever had. I can remember the first time Lydia saw a Cardinal, and the first time she saw an Oriole.

She was so thrilled to see that stuff! It was that way every time a new bird appeared.

Mary and Joel, the grand kids, and the great grand kids, are all the same way. They just love birds and nature.

Lydia was in the hospice program for two years. For those two years, she was able to sit and look out through the patio doors at the wildlife and at all the stuff she planted. All the trees were just little seedlings when she planted them. Now some of them are 60 to 70 feet high. Beautiful. The prettiest Maple tree in Mankato is out in the front yard. She planted that as about an eight-inch seedling. I guess it's really a pretty thing in the fall.

JOEL RIDING PATCHY WITH MARY HOLDING
THE REINS. GRANT OWEN AND SOME OF THE
OTHER NEIGHBORHOOD BOYS ARE IN THE
FRONT YARD, C. 1954

JUST THE WAY YOU ARE

———

This story might sound kind of fishy, but it's true!

One day, I was standing by the big sliding back door, looking out on the yard, and I said to Lydia, "You know with all the new kinds of medicine and procedures and all the stuff that's going on nowadays, maybe I should go and have an eye specialist take a look at that eye."

She came over to me, turned me around, gave me a big hug, and said, "I want you just the way you are. If you could see, you'd be different, and I don't want you different." She said, too, that if the procedure didn't turn out, I'd be disappointed, and she didn't want that either. She wanted things to be just exactly the way they were. That's the way that subject ended, and I never brought it up again.

THE END IN SIGHT

————

Lydia passed away on July 20, 2001.

She was in bed quite awhile. She had fallen and hurt her hip. She was suspicious that she had a broken bone, but wouldn't go to the hospital. She was also having big time problems with her throat. It finally got so that she couldn't swallow water, and she said she would go to the hospital and have Dr. Caruso check out her throat. He was a throat specialist that Harold had.

Before she went to the hospital she curled her hair, asked for the sack where she kept her cosmetics, and did her thing.

Mary was here and we had arranged for the Medivan to take her to the hospital. Mary and I followed behind in the Buick. Dr. Caruso opened her throat up, how I don't know, but that went along pretty good. At least she didn't complain.

She was having big time problems with her hip, though. They said she had to have an X-ray. The bone specialist checked out the X-ray and told us that the bone was broken off and slid up along side of the piece with the ball on it. She had been home with that broken hip for three weeks or more, struggling with it.

They said she needed surgery, but that she would never live through it. The doctor gave her options. She could go to a rest home or go back home. Mary and Joel were there. They went to get a cup of coffee and Lydia and I decided that she should come back home. She decided that I could take care of her like I had been. Joel and Mary came back in and we were talking back and forth and making plans to take Lydia back home, when she looked at Joel and looked at Mary kind of in a strange way, gasped a couple of times and was gone.

She suffered a lot in her lifetime. That's for sure. The nice thing though, was that she was sharp up till the last second. Her mind was perfect.

We had her cremated and had a simple church service, a memorial service. I have her here on the mantel in the living room. I think this spring we'll take her out to Joel and Dana's place and put her in the river. She told Joel exactly where she wanted to be put.

BLIND THE SECOND TIME

———

This is the 21st day of September, the year 2001. It's almost 7:00 am. The clocks will start striking in a minute or two. The first one to sound off will be the temperature clock Joseph gave me; then the talking clock; then the chime clock; then the bird clock; and then the striking clock on the mantle in the living room. They're all within 15 seconds of each other. I always had quite a time getting them in sync. Lydia and I used to struggle with that because I like to have things on time. I enjoy them all.

I can't remember what the temperature was. I think about 75 in here; 54 degrees outside.

I fed the birds in the dark. Put out fresh water. All the things that Lydia would like to have done. We always enjoyed this part of the morning, getting ready for the day.

She's been gone two months and one day. I am so *damned* lonesome. I don't know what to do to change it. I miss her so much. Keeping busy does help. I've been Colonel McClean. I scrubbed the bathrooms that don't need it, and vacuumed the rugs that don't need it. Just anything to keep busy.

ⅅ

Wes was here the other day and brought in goodies for me: cucumbers, pickles, bratwurst and more. They're sure givers.

This is a big, empty house. I just... I miss Lydia so much. I guess I feel a little better about it. Tuesday, she will be gone four months. It just doesn't seem real. You know, you expect those things. She was incapacitated for so long; over two years, and I knew what would happen, but when the time comes; well, you just would hope it would never come.

🖎

When I was typing, I hardly ever made a mistake. I know because Mary and I looked up the letters Lydia had saved, that I wrote her when she was in St. James. All those things just get me. If I say her name I want to cry.

I've spent a lot of time weeping this morning. I've been that way for many, many mornings. I just... I get so sad that I just... I'm so lonesome. That seems to be the thing with me. I'm so lonesome.

🖎

A student nurse, Judy Yang, called and would like to come here and learn how to be a nurse. I'm sure I can tell her all the good stuff they should do. Lydia told me, and I had enough experience with nurses too, to be able to tell her.

She seemed like a real nice kid. Super nice. Sharp. She seemed to be kind of anxious to come, and that's always nice too.

Some of those student nurses up on the floor in the hospital were really super, and some of them were not so super. Some of those guys that were going to school from the university there, were really, really, really good nurses. One guy especially, had super, super bedside manner.

I told her I had all kinds of little tips that people would like. It's the little things that people really enjoy having done. It isn't the big things.

🖎

I was just remembering when Mary and her friend John Williams came to Mankato on their new BMW motorcycle. It was a topic of conversation for some time. They thought I should go for a ride on it, so I went out and of course Lydia and Mary and Dana watched from inside. Lydia was kind of peeking out from behind the drape. Mary said, "What are you standing behind there for?" and Lydia said, "Well I don't want Daddy to see me watching him crawl aboard that bike."

𝒟

Today is Wednesday and I *think* it's the 6th of February. I had a kind of a full day today. Ellen stopped for a bit this morning before her Bible class, and Judy Yang, the student nurse, came. She was what I expected. She was a sharp cookie and really interested and interesting, both. I'm sure I can tell her a few things. I don't mean it that way, but, surely, I've had enough experience. She did seem to appreciate the opportunity to be here, so that was kind of fun.

Scott Albers, the guy from church, came and brought communion. I yakked with him for a while and then Wes Cornish came and brought me another hunk of bratwurst and some bread and butter pickles. I ate about half of that jar of pickles for supper tonight! They're real good.

𝒟

This is Sunday, April 21, 2002. I went to 8:00 mass with Dorothy Peterson and it was snowing to beat the devil when we came out of church. I talked to Joel and he said he thought they had at least two inches on the ground out there but the roads are clear.

I'm going to go out to Liza's place for Easter dinner at 5:00 this afternoon. They're going to come in and pick me up and we'll sail out there and meet some more of the clan. I went to Liza's husband's birthday party and met a big part of their family, but I guess there are some more of them coming to this one. She wanted me to come, so I thought I would.

𝒟

Today is Friday, July 26, 2002. Lydia died a year ago on the twentieth of July. I'm still having a hell of a time. I get so damned lonesome. I suppose it'll always be that way. She was the one with wings. She was a living angel, just something else. Miss Wonderful, and I sure did love her. I do have happy, happy memories but it still is hard to do the days.

She would enjoy the back yard. The flower garden is full of blossoms, I guess. The pansies are still blooming. I'm sure after the rain the grass has probably greened up. We had an inch and sure did need it. I'd like to get out there and do something, but I just... somehow I just don't have the poop.

♊

It is the last day of July 2002. Lydia's been gone a year and 11 days, a big hunk of a lonesome time. I sure miss her telling me what to do. Even to hear her tell me to straighten out the rug would be fun. I always did it, but always thought that it wasn't a necessary thing to do, but I guess it was.

I was thinking about Aunt Annie this morning. I wonder if I'll get a chance to thank her for the word she put in for me. Lydia and I had close to 60 years. I guess that's more than most people have. It still wasn't enough!

It's supposed to be a cooker out there today, up over 100, I guess. Joel stopped early this morning. He measured up the front window. He's going to replace a rotted board out there. Everything is getting old and rotten. I guess I fit that bill too.

He scared the life out of me when he came in. I was humped over the little table, pawing around for something. He opened the door and spoke and I could have jumped out of my shoes!

♊

I have willed my body to the University of Minnesota's medical department. I think I'm a pretty good-looking body actually, for an old fart. If all goes well, they will use me up in about 18 months and then will cremate me. After that, Joel, Mary, Dana and John can pick me up and they can put me in the river. It is a pretty spot out there, out on the point. Lydia and I can go down the river together.

I can still do more than 99% of the people that come around here. But I sure in hell can't do like I used to. Thank the Lord that Lydia wanted me to do everything. I am lucky. I sure had a good teacher and I sure miss her. I just... I know I'll never get over it, but that's the way the cookie crumbles.

⌁

I enjoy going to Dan's Barbershop. Lydia cut my hair for over 50 years, so it really was a big change.

She started cutting my hair before we were married. I tell the people in Dan's that it's pretty hard to do something with nothing 'cause I'm sure getting more and more bald as the years roll by. Have you heard the saying, "You can't have brains and hair?"

The other one is, "You can't grow grass in a manure pile."

I guess it depends on your perspective.

⌁

This is Saturday, August 24, 7:50 am. I imagine Joel and Dana will show sometime today. Joel's bike is out in the front yard. He took the Buick home last night after he finally gave up on his flat tire. One of the joys of riding a motorcycle, I guess, is having flat tires.

I just finished feeding the birds. One of those dirty hornets or wasps or whatever, dive-bombed me while I was out there. I'll have to have Liza check out the hummingbird feeder, and I think I'll have her put those bee guards in. I should have a "to do" list for her.

The kids will be here from Kentucky sometime today and will leave on Monday. Tom and Marsha, and her friend will arrive on Monday, so it will be a busy time.

⌁

I've got braunsweiger, and I've got some bratwurst too. You name it and I've got it. Pork chops and steak, pork cutlets, hamburger, liver, chicken. I had Mary set out beans and stuff for chili. I can make that in nothing flat.

This is getting to be Saturday night. I'm waiting for Joseph and the kids from Kentucky. I don't know when they'll get here. Joseph called when they were south of Madison, Wisconsin. It's a long old drive, that's for sure.

I put the tenderloin in at a quarter to seven. It's been in about 20 minutes. I was going to put the potatoes in too, but I think I'll do those in the microwave, maybe after they get here. It's a nice big tenderloin. I think I'll bake that about an hour and 5 or 10 minutes. It should be good.

𝔇

This is Monday, August 26, about 6:45 am. I've been up since 3:30. The kids are sleeping yet. They're going to take off today. I don't know what time. They got here about 9:30 Saturday night and we went out to eat yesterday after church. We came back home, and sat around and chewed the fat.

Mary called. She'll be home today.

Tom called. He'll be in the Cities at 2:00 this afternoon. Marsha and her friend will pick him up. He said they were going to come right here after they picked him up, so they should be here by 6:00, even if they fiddle around. I'll do that rack of ribs and we'll have some baked potatoes and salad.

I don't know if Joel and Dana will come. I invited them. Anyhow, round and round she goes. Everything's gone real well so far. I told Lacey the Buick was hers yesterday. She was quite happy to say the least. Quite a bit to give a kid.

𝔇

I did Lutheran Bible study group this morning. Five ladies and me; a rose among the thorns! They're a real interesting group. I *think* I fit in there. I'm comfortable and they say they are. I don't think they do anything different with me there. I told them I didn't want to screw up their meeting. I asked them how come I was the only man there, and they had all kinds of answers to that question.

I enjoy the bible study real much. I just finished a book, *Civilization Before Greece and Rome*, and there was a lot of bible history preceding Greece and Rome. I really, really enjoyed that book. It was about 500 to 600 pages.

𝕯

I'm listening to Carl And The Country Dutchmen. I think this is the best old time band in existence. Carl plays the accordion. I really, really would enjoy talking to him. I probably will some day. I just love his music. I can tell him from anybody else, and I listen to a lot of old-time music. Just listen to that tuba!

I like to tape on cassette tapes like I'm doing right now. I've taped storms and part of a heart attack and angina attacks. I tape when I feel good and when I feel rotten. I must enjoy hearing my own voice! I really do enjoy taping.

There was an article printed in the *St. Paul Pioneer Press* on February 25. A guy from Chicago wrote in, explaining how to play the game of Mumbly-peg. The article appeared in what they call *The Bulletin Board*. Then on March 1, someone wrote an article for *The Bulletin Board*, telling about a young man with his Seeing Eye dog cruising the streets of Mankato. She was in the sixth grade at the time. It must have been when I first got Art because she said I was handsome!

𝕯

I had the Lutheran Bible study group here this morning. Eight ladies and me. We meet every Wednesday at 9:00 am. They're really a nice group. If you didn't know, you wouldn't be able to tell the difference between the Lutheran and the Catholic bible study. I have had both of them here now.

We had coffee and they have Christmas breads, cookies, and all that good stuff before and during the meeting. After the meeting they sit around and chew the fat. They really enjoyed being here, and I enjoyed having them here.

They liked the old house and this room especially, with the nice big eight-foot sliding glass doors looking out onto a real nice back yard. It looks like you are up north with the pine trees, the birch, the maple, the birds, and what-have-you. I feed and keep water out for the birds and anything that comes along. Joel thought there were deer tracks out in the snow, so they have been around I guess. We do have everything, squirrels, chipmunks, coon, opossum, rabbits, many kinds of birds, not in number but in variety. The bird population has gone down hill in the last few years.

Everything is covered with nice, clean snow. You know, when people look out the back door and just in general conversation talk about what they see, I see it just as well as they do, and that way I really don't miss anything.

I love the bible, and I always come away from the meeting with something. The discussion today was on prayer. I pray a lot for this auto-biography to turn out good.

There's an archeologist that's going to do a program on a dig in Jerusalem, or near Haifa? He did a dig there and he's going to put a program on in one of the Lutheran churches. I kind of think it is the one across from the Franklin School. Somebody read it over at the bible study meeting and I said, "Well, I'd kind of like to go to that," and Ellen said, "We'll go." It was a done deal as far as she was concerned. We'll see anyhow. I wouldn't want to go feeling like I do now. I should keep busy. Maybe I'd feel better.

ℝ

I made myself a nice, big, juicy beef hamburger for dinner tonight; more than a quarter pound. I used some of Lydia's seasoning. I think I'll have Liza make a couple of batches of Lydia's seasoning for me to give away for Christmas. Anyhow, I had a big hamburger and hash brown potatoes, a little salad and a piece of pumpkin pie that Ellen brought over.

Ellen brought the pumpkin pie over and I had a couple of Liza's Christmas cookies too, so you can see I am not starving.

❦

As soon as the rhubarb was big enough, I went out and pulled some for a batch of wine. I pulled it, trimmed the root end and the leaf off, weighed it and brought it in the house. I had 17 pounds of rhubarb. I washed it, cut it up, and chucked it into a big, 10-gallon crock, fermenting jar. I poured boiling hot water on, enough to cover, and dumped in 25 pounds of sugar. I stirred it up good and covered the jar with a big dishtowel. I let it set for a few days until the rhubarb started to get mushy. Then Joel and I got another big 10-gallon crock, dipped the juice from the rhubarb pulp out of the jar and strained it through the dishtowel, into the other crock. When we got all of the rhubarb into the towel, we wound it up and really, really squeezed the remaining juice out, big time. We poured four containers of Welch's pure grape juice into the rhubarb mixture, and then added a couple of those little packs of champagne yeast, and stirred it into the juice. We covered it up with a clean dishtowel and let it start to ferment. It really went to town big time! It smelled the whole house up with a good smell.

I don't remember how many days we left it in the fermenting jar. After it started to die down a bit, I had Joel set the crock up on the table and we siphoned it into a carboy. I think we had to add a little water to it to fill the carboy up. We put an airlock on the top of the carboy and let 'er go to town!

❦

This is the 21st of March, the first day of spring. It's hard not to listen to the war news from Iraq. It goes on and on. I just hope it ends in a hurry. And then the big job will come. You can bet on that. There are so many different factions involved in that deal. It's unreal. They've been fighting one another for centuries. I was surprised to hear that Baghdad is really a big modern town, with five million people, very sophisticated, and the people are well educated.

It sounds like the war effort is going along pretty well. They've got B-52's in the air now, having taken off from England, and apparently they have a payload that's something else. I'm not familiar with the stuff they carry, but from the news, it must be really devastating when they start dropping their stuff. Tonight sounds like it's going to be the start of the big bombing session.

⊅

It's Thursday. We had a big time tornado storm Monday night. We had rain Tuesday. I guess we had rain yesterday too. But today has been without rain, 85-90 degrees, somewhere in there. There's a breeze out, but the humidity was high, so I suppose if you were out in it, it'd be kind of poopy.

I've got it really, really great in here. It's air-conditioned and with the overhead fan in the back room here, it's really, really nice! Nobody could have it better. It's such a nice home. It's old. Even the glaze on the plates is wearing off! Everything is old, old, old. But you know, we have everything here.

Liza kind of gets a kick out of being here. She said, "If you can find it, it's here." I like it that way too. I try to keep the inventory up. If we run out of something, I like to refill it right away. That's the way it always was.

I have quite a nice variety of birds, and chipmunks, squirrels, and hummingbirds. You name it and they're out there. Not in big numbers, but they're there.

Ellen and Yogi were just here. She picked up one of her dishes that she had brought stuff over to me in. She brought a different kind of rice dish. Basmati? It's different, and it is real good. I had, I'm sure at least three meals out of what she brought over. She brought chicken over yesterday. She brought cake with the chicken, a big piece of cake.

Everybody is good to me. They bring lots of stuff. I have so much stuff to eat, I don't get a chance to cook, and strange as it may seem to others, I do like to cook.

The recipes I use are probably pretty simple. My technique is good. I had a good teacher. Lydia let me cook and I helped. Oh, not always, but after retiring, I always helped. I always cleaned up. I am good at that!

I know when things are hot. I put my hand on them. Honestly. If I cook something in the little oven, I reach in and feel of it. I can tell when it's done.

I make chili, meatloaves, ribs, fish, soup, and you name it. Garbage soup is one of my favorites. I empty all the leftover crap in the refrigerator into a bowl and, usually it's pretty good.

Measuring is rough, but if I'm measuring a liquid, I use a measuring cup over the sink so if I spill or slop, it goes into the sink.

Most of the things I make are things Lydia had me do, when she was in bed.

I get "meat hungry", and when I do, I whip out a big juicy hunk of venison burger. I don't have any beef in the freezer now, but I have venison. It's really, really good venison sausage, seasoned just right. I make patties out of that and make a big juicy burger on my George Foreman. That thing really works good for me. I can and do cook everything on it – fish, steaks, and burger. I haven't made a grilled cheese lately. I should do that. I really enjoy them, and it works just slicker 'n a whistle on that thing.

I've got the poached egg situation down now too. Ellen picked up a single egg poacher in the thrift store that works great. Seventeen seconds. "One and two and three and..." I count or time everything. With my burgers on the George Foreman, as soon as I hear it start sizzling, I time it on my talking calendar. I use that timer a lot. I'm lucky to be able to do that stuff, and I like to do it.

I bought another big rack of ribs. I'll have to make an occasion and feed somebody with them. It's really nothing to do. I cut the ribs up and chuck 'em into the pressure cooker. Then I season them with Lydia's seasoning and put in about a cup, or maybe a cup and a half of water. I seal that baby up, and bring it up to a good time boil.

Lydia said when steam pushes out of that outlet about a foot above the cooker; you can slap the gauge on it. You let it come up to heat again, maybe a minute, and then turn the dial straight down on the stove. Then I cook it for about 22 minutes. When they come out of there, they're just perfect. Just super flavored. Then I lay them out in one of those ceramic baking dishes, open up the old jar of barbecue sauce, dump it into my hand and smear it around on the ribs; be sure to cover them all, and stick them in the oven. I bake them at about 325 degrees for 35 to 40 minutes.

You know something? They're just perfect if I do say so, and I do. Really, they are just scrumptious. It's fun to be able to do that kind of stuff. I had a good teacher. Lydia expected me to do everything. It's lucky for me that she did. I'd never be able to live like this if she hadn't been that way. That's for darn sure.

I've been trying to get somebody to look at the shingles on the house. I talked to Joel just a little while ago and he thought we should be able to get by with just repairing that dormer out in front where the ice backed up and kind of screwed the shingles up. The rest of the house, I think, looks pretty good. Everybody that looks at it says it does.

I called two guys, and one guy answered my call. Nowadays you have a hell of a time getting anybody to do anything! It's just unreal! So we'll see what he comes up with.

You know, I did all of that yakking in one shot up to this point. Pretty gassy!

⌀

Time does pass. The days do go. Sunday, Lydia will be gone two years. In one way, the time has gone fast and in another way, it's dragged. I do have a rough time. I just – I get so damned lonesome. I should think more about the good times we had, I guess. We sure had lots of those. We had a super, super time together.

✍

Another day in the book. It's Friday, July 18, getting along towards 7:00 p.m. Harold came over this afternoon. We had a short one, visited for a while, and he took off for home. Joel was here for lunch at noon. It's kind of nice when he comes to break up the day. Ellen brought crab and shrimp salad that I had for lunch. She got sweet corn, and I had two ears of corn for supper tonight. Both the salad and the corn were just super. Super, super. I just really, really enjoyed both of them.

These were nice full ears of real tender, juicy corn. And fresh picked!

Liza will come early tomorrow morning at around 8:00. I don't know what I'll have her do. I guess maybe I'll have her make a batch of cookies. I'll have her check everything, the tomatoes, the pansies, and the herb garden. She does a super job on everything.

I got quite a bit of mail today. I heard from the bank, and a thank you card for a graduation present, two tapes from the Seeing Eye and one from *Reader's Digest*. I really enjoy *Reader's Digest*. It's really interesting. It's like reading a magazine. You hate to lay it down. I get a lot of books and magazines from the American Foundation for the Blind, including the four-track tape player. It sure is nice.

I think I'll button this up for the day. Have a good one!

✍

Today is Saturday, July 19. Tomorrow will be two years since Lydia passed away. She was so little. It was unreal. I was just thinking of the pain she must have gone through, having a broken hip for, it had to be at least three weeks, unwilling to go to the doctor. She never did go for her hip. She went for her throat. She couldn't swallow anything anymore. Her life seemed to be just full of miseries, one thing after another.

I sure miss her.

It promises to be a pretty nice day. I just fed the birds and put fresh water in the birdbath. It's about 60 degrees. I wonder what the day will bring. I wonder if the guy will come and look at the roof of the house.

Later...

It's sure shitty sitting around here alone. I've got it good, but it's still shitty.

Another nice, nice day today. Joel and Dana worked around the house till noon, and then they took off on the bike and did about 150 miles, cruising around, and went back home.

I tried to call John and Mary and I guess they're probably doing the same thing, cruising on the bike.

Liza was here this morning, at 8:00. I had her go to the store and pick up some goodies.

I had the guy look at the shingles on the house. He crawled up on top of the roof and said that we had hail damage up there, that the shingles on the west and on the south side have been beat with the hail. This guy has been shingling for 30 years. He's licensed and the whole bag, and he said, "That's hail damage," so as far as I'm concerned, it's hail damage.

Later still...

It's almost 8:00 pm. Another day is in the book. I racked that carboy of rhubarb and grape wine. It tastes good too and it isn't through working yet. On the hydrometer, it read 1.050, and on the 3rd of July it read 1.060. It isn't real, real sweet, but it is sweeter than the wines I've ever been involved with. It is still working so it'll eat up more of that sugar. I can't remember what color Liza said it was. Isn't that dumb?

It's Wednesday, about 8:00 am, and I feel pretty good today. I've been up since before 5:00.

We've got a storm brewing. If we have a big time rainstorm going through, I like to record the rain and thunder. I can see the flash of the lightning if it is fairly close, and I guestimate how far away it is by the time it takes to hear the thunder, usually by counting seconds. I do enjoy hearing a storm come up. They usually start off in the west and work themselves to the east in this area.

Monday we had tornadoes go through here. Apparently at least four touched down. They measure them nowadays so they know what category they fall in. These were "one" and "two" grade. "Three" is one that does big time damage. The one that hit St. Peter five years ago was a category three, and it really tore the town up, really, really bad. It was wide. One of these that just went through here Monday was only a few yards wide, I guess. They can be up to miles wide when they start sweeping the countryside.

The thunder has been rumbling off to the southeast, as I'm sitting here looking straight north. The radio is forecasting the storm to hit here within minutes. I was going to sweep the deck and put out seed for the birdies but I guess I'll wait until that thing goes over. The weatherman said it was moving fast, but we'll see.

There's another little crack of thunder. If it gets close, I'm going to tape it. It's been rolling for an extended time and still rumbling. I guess in the old days they used to call that chain lightening? I don't think it's raining here yet. It doesn't sound like it anyhow.

I'm out in the doorway now. It's just starting to rain and sounds like big drops. There's a little crack of thunder. That was straight north of here. The rain is picking up. They said there was hail coming too. I sure hope that doesn't come about. It'll knock my nice tomatoes all to hell. I had three little ones yesterday, and I guess there are two or three more that should be ripe today if we get a little sunshine.

Boy, it's really starting to rain big time now. It's been a funny year with the storms. We've sure had many of them.

The thunder is moving to the east. It's quite a ways from here I think. I haven't seen any lightening at all.

The rain is kind of letting up. The thunder is far away, to the north, and a little to the west. We were lucky the other night that the storm completely missed us.

That one was fairly close to here, and I still didn't see any flash of lightning. I can hear thunder way, way to the west, so there's more coming. THERE, I saw lightning. Now we'll see how far away it was. There's another flash. That's a long ways away. The thunder was several seconds coming.

I get a kick out of doing this crap.

※

I just finished a big glass of that wine we held out when we racked it the last time, a week or 10 days ago. It's a real full-bodied, sweet wine, sweeter than I like. It should be good when it mellows out. I'd say it tastes pretty darn good right now. I suppose if you'd bottle it now it would blow the corks off. It hasn't started to clear yet, but Joseph said to just leave it and maybe rack it another time and if it doesn't clear, to put in Bentonite.

※

The wine was kind of cloudy so we added a water and Bentonite mixture to it, and that cleared it real well.

After the wine in the carboy was cleared, the cloudiness gone and it quit working (there were no little bubbles on the top of the wine) Mary and I bottled it. I scalded the bottles in scalding hot water and Mary and I filled them. I'd hand a bottle to Mary. She'd measure the wine into the bottle, set it up on the table, I'd hand her another bottle and so forth.

After we drained the carboy and filled the bottles, we corked them. Mary would throw the cork into the corker and steer it over on top of the bottle and I'd scrunch it down, push it away, and do another one. After that, she wiped off all the bottles and labeled them with labels that Joseph had made. They said, "Grandpa Footner's Rhubarb and Grape Wine." They were real nice labels that made it look real professional.

⅌

The First Lady didn't amount to anything this year. It was fertilized and watered and it had tender loving care. The peppers didn't amount to anything either. There are half a dozen peppers on, I guess, and there should be half a hundred, or more than that! They should be just red with peppers!

Maura brought some red peppers. I bit the end off one and it is hot, that's for danged sure. Hot, hot! You know you get some of those things and take them straight, and it darned near strangles you!

We bought some salsa and I'd say it's just like homemade. It's real, real, good.

Caroline was making salsa yesterday. She makes real good stuff, and they're sure generous with it. That's for sure. Every so often they bring me a case of pint jars of beans, carrots, potatoes, and what have you; beef roast for hot beef sandwiches, and roasted turkey for turkey sandwiches, chicken soup, salsa, pickles. It's unreal.

I'm feeling real sorry for myself this morning. The last few days have been rough. I miss Lydia so much. I suppose the holidays coming is a part of it and... ah yah. Life goes on.

I'll bet not very long after Lydia and I were married, I started writing individual Christmas letters to friends and relatives – 25, 30 letters or more, every year. Everyone seemed to enjoy them, so I did it. I get by the easy way now with taping my Christmas letter. Mary runs them off and does all the hard work.

⅌

The little talking clock didn't work for a while. I banged it a couple good ones and it came to life again. That works with a lot of stuff you know. The microwave went bad; I bet it was 6, 8, 10 months ago. I whopped it a good one and it came to life. No more problem. I did the same thing with the little oven, and the icemaker too. That went on the fritz, and I banged it one. Now it's working good.

I talked to Dorothy and she'll take me to church tomorrow so I'll pray for all you guys! I'll pray for myself too. I probably need it more than anybody.

෯

There must be a squirrel going up the middle post on the sliding glass door here. I'll betcha-by-golly he's going up and into the window feeders. The hummingbirds are still here. Mary saw them this morning. So are the bees, the little devils. I thought it would be too cold and they'd be gone, but she said there were bees out along one of the hummingbird feeders.

෯

Today is Sunday, December 7, 2003 getting on toward 9:00 a.m. I didn't go to church today. I started feeling better about the time church started. I was going to start a to-do list and I forgot what I was going to have Liza do. I didn't like any of the books I got from the library.

෯

Today is December 11, 2003. Yesterday, Liza and I bottled 49 bottles of Zinfandel grape wine. I'm planning to give most of it away for Christmas. Everything went real, real well. Basically, we used the same procedure I did with the rhubarb and grape; only the Zinfandel was made from a kit that was purchased at the hobby store here in Mankato. It was a real high-grade kit that made excellent wine.

෯

The batch of Zinfandel wine Liza and I did two weeks before Christmas is almost gone. I intended to give it away, and between drinking it and giving it away, I think there are only four small bottles left from that batch of 35 small one's and 14 regular ones. The small bottle holds two nice glasses of wine. I don't know how many glasses the big one holds.

Joseph did the labels and sent them to me from Kentucky. They really added something. They're real professional looking, and it's really, really good wine too.

I can still do a lot of the work involved in making the wine. I sterilize the fermenting jar and sterilize the bottles. I can't see and read the labels and I wouldn't be able to fill the bottles, but I can cork them. Like always, I can tell people what to do! That's something I excel at! Most of the time they respond. I'm going to make another batch too, in the not too distant future. Its kind of fun to have something like that going. We've got it down now so it's pretty easy going.

It's a real good conversation piece. That's for sure. I had a bible study group from my church here one session and we opened the session with a glass of wine. It seemed to me that it just fit.

☙

I'm going to make another batch of rhubarb and grape wine as soon as the rhubarb is big enough this spring, Lord willin'. I have to qualify that all the time now – the Lord willin'. I have a nice growth of rhubarb out there, real good stuff. We've had that here almost from day one. I'm kind of looking forward to spring and it isn't far off. I suppose it's only about 75 days or so till the snow will all be gone. We don't have snow now and it's the 6th, or 7th of January, 2004 already. Uffda! That'll make me 90 years old in June. Unreal!

☙

It's almost 9:00 pm, January 17, 2004. No snow, no ice, no nothin'. In fact, I guess the grass out in back here is even kind of green. That's unreal for this time in Minnesota. Spring isn't far away.

Everybody's going to be taking off for cruises and trips to the islands. Maybe I should take a trip. You know, for me to take a trip alone really wouldn't be all that hard. Everybody just jumps through a hoop for a poor, old blind man. I'd probably get a chance to get up and ride with the pilots!

I should talk to Scott Albers, my good friend who flies for Comair out of Cincinnati. He called me just a couple days ago, from Cincinnati. He's getting lots of flying time. He does a commuter hookup for American, I think.

I made arrangements to have Dorothy pick me up to go to church tomorrow, so I'll pray for all you guys, and pray for myself too. I need big time help. I've been asking the Good Lord to help me with this autobiography, so I hope it goes well.

Caroline and Harold will be taking off on their cruise out of Miami on the 3rd of February, and Joel, Dana, Mary, and John will be taking off for the Caribbean. They'll be flying into St. Thomas, and then to St. John's, I guess, on the 13th of February.

I have an appointment to see the good doctor, Stephanie Putzier, Wednesday at 11:40. She's a good doctor, and she doesn't think she can walk on water.

$$\mathcal{D}$$

I went to church yesterday with Dorothy and Carol. Dorothy's birthday is in August and she'll be 90. Carol is 88. So, there were an 89, 89, and 88-year-old sitting in that pew. Three old farts. That's a lot of years if you add them up!

$$\mathcal{D}$$

So far, I'd say the wine we've made has been real good. Everybody seems to enjoy it. I plan to keep on making it as long as I can do the job. If I can't do it, like sterilizing the fermenting jar, sterilizing the bottles, and carrying stuff up out of the basement – if I couldn't do that kind of stuff, I wouldn't make it. Period.

I can't lift the big heavy stuff any more, but that's about it. I like to do the corking. I have to have a big hand in making it, or it'll end. But it is a good topic of conversation and people do enjoy it.

$$\mathcal{D}$$

This is the last day of the month, January 31, about 10 after 8:00 or so, in the morning. Harold is going to pick me up at around 9:00. I'm going to go to the doctor and have a few things checked out. I have an appointment for 9:40. It's been quite a long time since I've had anybody take a look. It must be 8 or 10 months, getting up toward a year. I feel pretty good this morning, really. I guess it's pretty much true that when you are going to go to the doctor, you start feeling better.

Tomorrow the kids take off for Barbados. I'm sure they're really anxious to get on the way. They have a layover in New York City and then fly directly to Barbados. Mary's high school friend, Denise is going to pick them up I guess, which should make it really nice.

Maura, what a good person! She's really a sweetheart. I'm surrounded by people like that!

I told Maura that I'm a Footner, and they are an egotistical lot. All of them. Well, my Grandpa, Harry; he liked Harry. That's for sure. I know my dad was a smart aleck, and I was a smart aleck. Tom and Dick have more ego than even I do! Joel is more mild. Mary is so-so. Lydia was humble. She never put on airs.

I'm real happy to be living here in the old house with all the old things around, and believe me, they are getting old. A lot of stuff has to be replaced off and on. It kind of drains the bank account, but I'm lucky to be able to stay here alone. I do appreciate it. I have lots of great people coming in to help. I know I have more people come in a week, than a lot of old people have in a year. I have lots of company, if I don't have them in person; I have them on the telephone. I enjoy talking to people.

Today is February 6, 2004, 4:00 pm. It's the same old rigmarole. I'm sitting out in the back room looking out on the snowbound back yard. Everything is covered with a new snowfall, about two inches or maybe three. The twentieth of July, Lydia will be gone three years.

I find myself leaning over, asking her questions. It just is unreal that she isn't sitting in that chair to my left. We were lucky, I know. We had over 20 years in retirement together. Lots of people don't get 20 years, *period*. She would have been 91, February 22. It's unreal how time passes.

All the young people are a-comin' and a-goin'. Even the old people. Caroline and Harold are on the high seas right at the moment, on a cruise that will take them down to Barbados and then back up along South America. Harold was sure looking forward to it. Caroline was too. Harold especially, because he hadn't been aboard a ship since he was in the Navy. He saw big time action. He has an interesting story to tell, boy. I keep encouraging him. I should tape him! I bet he'd let me! I know more about him and his time in service than anybody, and it's interesting!

I'm sure my neighbor will shovel the sidewalk tonight. He hasn't started at it yet or at least I haven't heard it. I don't know if he'll do it with a shovel or with a snow blower. It's about two or three inches of snow and I think it's kind of wet, the stuff that would be heavy on the shovel. We need it. That's for sure. We need moisture.

✾

Someone asked me once what was the most beautiful thing I had seen. All the beautiful things I would expound on would be in nature, I guess. I know we have a maple tree out in the front yard that Lydia planted as a seedling and now it's huge. It's a real big tree, and in the fall, it has that beautiful red leaf, the prettiest tree in Mankato.

See, I see all that stuff through other people's eyes, and really, I miss very little. I always was well informed on everything. In the time of year when the roses bloom, I know that the Seven Sisters climbing rose is beautiful.

I have the advantage over lots of blind people because I *have* seen. I actually know what things and people and all look like. Like with the birds out on the deck, the birds that I feed and water year around, if someone is here and can't identify the bird, if they accurately describe it,

I'd say 9 times out of 10 I know, and I'm able to tell them what kind of bird it is.

℘

I have five little girls that come to see me. In the summer, they come almost every day.

There's Lily, Annie, Mattie, Eliza, Jessica, and occasionally Benjamin comes along too. He's a brother to a couple of them. They never stay very long. They just come in and shoot the breeze a little bit, and take off. They don't meander around. They tend to stay pretty much by the back door. They're really, really something. I just love to have them come.

Some of the kids have a fort out in the back yard too. They take branches and leaves, and all that stuff, and lay them out in a kind of a hideout like kids do. There's been as many as seven of them out in that fort at one time. They rake and chop and scrape, and everything for their fort.

There's one kid that likes the white pine out there. It's about 60 or 70 feet high and I'm sure it's a real good tree to climb. Of course everybody chases those kids out of the yard, but not me. I tell them to just leave the kids alone. If they fall, so be it. Last fall, there was a kid, 13 or 14 years old, who climbed that white pine. Mary and Joe were here and they watched him do it. He went way up high and was coming back down, probably 15 feet from the ground or so. All of a sudden he came down and lit on his back. You could hear the thud in the house here. It was big time.

Joseph and Mary dashed out to help. Joseph was trained, so he knew what to do. He made him lay still until they knew what cooked with him. They brought him to. It had knocked the wind out of him, but I guess he didn't break any bones or anything. He must have lit just right! I still would let the kids climb. Nowadays, everybody shags them out of the yards. They don't want them around.

They said, "He'll sue you."

I said, "Sue a beggar and catch a louse." I like to have them out and about.

⁊

Note to Liza:

Would you sweep the deck and wipe out the birdbath? You can get a jolt off that birdbath if you do it wrong. If you're going to do much messing around with it, unplug it from the house. I know from experience. I didn't unplug it and I was messing around where it's plugged into the extension cord. It was wet and I really got a good one, with the sparkling eyes and all!

⁊

Today is Sunday, February 22, 2004, Lydia's birthday. She would have been 91 today. Too bad the good have to die.

⁊

I have two grandchildren and three great grandchildren. Mary is the source. She had two boys, Joseph and Jeff. Joseph, the oldest, has three; two girls and a little boy; Lacey, Alisha, and Glen. Lacey is 17, Alisha 15 and Glen is four. All smart. Sharp as a tack.

Joseph works for UPS. He just got word that he got a great big   promotion out of the blue. No inkling at all. He's perfect for that company. He's 39 years old, and real well physically. He's strong, aggressive, and intelligent. He has a good background for the job. He is in avionics. I look for him to go onward and upward. I told him that too, that he had a good chance to be big time in UPS. He's exactly what they want, in my book. Of course, I'm kind of biased, but I think I know enough about people.

⁊

I called Daisy to get Becky's number and chinned with her a little while. Then I called and left a message for Becky, and she called me back. Becky is my niece, my sister Daisy's youngest daughter. She is a paralegal and works for Mike Hatch, the State Attorney General. She and her friend Steve are both good musicians. Steve plays a super piano and Becky plays piano, guitar, keyboards and the whole bag. Becky plays gigs all around the Twin Cities and elsewhere and they play together some too.

I had a super, super conversation with her. I just really enjoy yakking with her. Somehow, she kind of understands me, I think. And of course we both love music. Sounds like she's doing pretty darned good right now, too. I wish she and Steve would come here. I know we'd have fun.

She likes my kind of music, but she isn't just stuck on one thing. She likes everything. That's me too. I like everything. But somehow the music I listen to now, it just... so much of it reminds me of Lydia, and when I hear it, I get so sad. I just sit here and cry. I can't help it. I miss her so much.

Maybe it's the same for everybody. I don't know. It probably is. They all are wiping tears away.

It will soon be time for me to sack it up and call it a day.

It's supposed to go to 65 degrees tomorrow. That should be pretty nice. It was in the 60's today. I didn't get out but a couple of minutes. Maybe tomorrow, I'll get out and scratch around. I'm going to go to church. I talked to Dorothy and she'll pick me up.

I had a hunk of a great big juicy pork roast for supper. Potatoes, carrots and onions. It was super, super good. I don't care who did it. They couldn't do it any better!

The sad part is, I like to cook. If I didn't, I wouldn't be gaining so much weight, maybe!

This is the end of the day, the 22nd of March. My brother Dick's birthday would have been the 25th of March. Funny, how I remember those birthdays. They were always a big deal in our life when we were kids.

𝕯

It sounds like the Kutcher wedding on the fifth of June, is really going to be big time. Maura's busy getting bridesmaid dresses lined up and they have people coming in from New Zealand, New York and all over, with 150 people invited. It's going be held in the Minnesota Historical Society building.

Stephanie Putzier is on vacation, so another doctor read my CAT scan. According to him, there's no problem. There's a degeneration of the brain that goes along with old age, I guess. I think that shimmering deal has let up a little bit and I wonder if it isn't that additional heart medicine I'm taking.

I am having a rough time on short-term memory. I set something down, and turn away from it, and then wonder where it is.

I'm sure the sun is shining right now. The temp is supposed to go to 45 degrees and we're supposed to have big time wind, 30 miles an hour. Even with the temperature up, with snow on the ground and the wind, it's chilly. It's penetrating. I should feed the birdies, take a shower, wash the dishes, take my pills, and brush my teeth.

🕊

This is Tuesday night, getting on toward 8:00 pm. It's the 9th of March. Liza was here, did her thing and took off. Maura called and will pick up this tape. Boy I'm getting terrible! I can't remember when she said she'd come. Yuck! I hate that! There isn't a hell of a lot I can do about it though. My short-term memory is kaput! That shimmering has lessened some. It isn't near as bad as it was. Like right now, I don't see anything at all. That's real good.

🕊

I'm going to have a big time birthday party Saturday, June 12, 2004. I'll be 90 years old. Unreal! I'm going to have an open house here, at my house. We've reserved a 20 x 20 tent and five tables, 100 chairs, and a Porta-Potty. Liza will bring two picnic tables, Craig will furnish the garbage cans, and the Elite Steak and Chops Shop will furnish the meat for hot beef sandwiches. They will cook the meat and deliver it.

John is going to bring Captain Ken's Baked Beans. Liza is going to do the salad, the same kind of salad she had for her daughter Tiffany's graduation. Good stuff! We'll have pickles and birthday cake and pop or lemonade and coffee. No beer, no booze.

All my friends and relatives are invited. The plan is for 200 and I hope there's 1000! I know lots of people, from work and church and neighborhood and relatives. I hope the Sandmeyer clan shows in number. I just hope we have good weather and that it turns out to be a happy time.

One thing missing. Lydia. She never enjoyed stuff like that. She didn't enjoy having her picture taken or parties. Well, she liked parties but she didn't want to be the main one in anything. She was humble.

⚘

It's just a little after 10:00 in the morning. I went to 8:00 mass. It was sprinkling a little bit when I left home here and was raining when I came back. Dorothy Peterson took me to church. We have a new assistant priest down there. I thought he did real well. He's a young guy. This is his first assignment. He graduated from the university here, went to a seminary in Winona, and then finished his "priestly duties" in Chicago. I'd say he's a pretty good speaker. I think everything went pretty well.

I was wandering around with no religion really. As a kid, I was a Methodist, and when I started going with Lydia, she was a Catholic. I wasn't pressured in any way to join the church, but I did. I took instructions from a young priest, Father Dailey. I did my thing, and he baptized me. He baptized Art too, my Seeing Eye dog. Father Dailey up and died awhile back too.

I have honestly enjoyed church. We always went to all of the holidays and the commitments to the church, and I especially enjoy it now. I have a church hearing aid that picks up real well so I don't miss anything, even when the good Father whispers up on the altar.

I attended a Bible study group at St. John's during the winter of 2002 and early 2003. The group varied from half a dozen to 15. For the last session, I invited them to my home and they did come. There were 14 of us. It was really a nice meeting. The first thing I did was serve them all a glass of the homemade wine. Even those that said they didn't drink wine drank it. It seemed to kind of loosen the group up and it was a real pleasant evening. I had coffee and cake after the meeting, and a lot of BS. I did enjoy the group. Well, I enjoy the bible. I have been reading some of it on tapes.

I have also been reading Wallace Stegner. He wrote about the early days in the Western United States, about the people and the country. I really enjoyed one of his books, *A Big Rock Candy Mountain*.

I enjoy ancient history, especially. I have done Chinese heritage and Egyptian heritage and the story of the Indian populations in South America, the Aztecs and the Mayans.

I have done quite a bit of reading on a four-track tape player. The books and the tape player are all provided by the American Foundation for the Blind, out of Louisville, Kentucky.

✹

I've just been singing along with "Just the Thought of You". It Makes me think of my Lydia. The songs just kill me, but I still love them.

✹

Today is the 22nd. Harold was here this afternoon. Caroline is having big time problems with her aching back. She's so much like Lydia it's unreal. All her aches and pains are almost a mirror of Lydia's. The only thing different is that she had a cancer and Lydia never did.

It's hard boy. Hard, hard. I feel for the two of them, Caroline and Harold. You have to go through those sessions to really appreciate what it's like. Barb Kraft came over to me when we were at the reunion, and that's what she said. "You understand what it's like for me," and I do. Her legs were paralyzed from a car accident when she was driving home to see her dad on Father's Day. She's gutsy and aggressive, and everything about her is really, really good. She just doesn't hold still for anything, and I'd like to think I didn't either. Lydia expected me to do everything, and I did, so consequently, I'm able to live alone here.

I still need somebody to read stuff to me and pick up stuff that I've lost on the floor. I wear Lydia's wedding ring and I discovered that thing gone. I was almost in a panic to find the dumb thing. I flipped chairs over, and dug and scraped around. I finally gave up. I knew it was in the house. Isn't that dumb? Ellen came over, and she was sitting in the chair off the end of the bed and I told her about losing that ring – that I had looked all over for it, and dumped chairs and all that kind of stuff.

All of a sudden she said, "Oh! There's your ring, laying on the floor there," and she went over and picked it up. I was really, really tickled with that, I'll tell ya. I do enjoy wearing it. I fumble with it all the time. Something to play with, you know. But that's the kind of seeing I need. I can do a lot of stuff, but I do need eyes once in awhile.

$\mathcal{D}$

I guess there are worse things than being blind. Well, I know there are! I have been lucky.

We've seen it from scratch really, from horse and buggy to today when everything is so fast. We lived through the beginning of electricity, the beginning of automobiles, the beginning of radio, television; it goes on and on. All of that started up in our lifetime. Computers came into being just about the time I retired. It's hard to imagine.

It's funny how you can put a lifetime down on a tape in a few minutes. Lots of water went under the bridge in those 60 years that Lydia and I were together. Many, many happy times. There was never anything Lydia and I couldn't do together. Nothing. We were as independent as a hog on ice. We had sad times too, but we were together, and together we could do anything.

Written under contract by Larry R. Hutson, based entirely on information provided by Harry Footner.

PEOPLE IN MY LIFE

———

Mary Rogich – my daughter, lives in St. Paul, MN. She is retired after working at Hibbing Taconite Co. for twenty-six years.

John Williams – Mary's partner, is a truck driver.

Joel Footner – my son, is a carpenter for J. F. Johnson Construction.

Dana Peterson – Joel's partner, is a beautician at J. C. Penney. They live near Mapleton MN and have a beautiful place by the river.

Joseph Simonson – Mary's oldest son lives in LaGrange, KY and works for UPS.

Yvonne Simonson – Joseph's wife also worked for UPS but is sewing now.

Glen, Lacey and Alisha (Ali) Simonson – Joseph's children. The girls go to school in Litchfield MN and live with their mother, Karen. They spend some holidays and summers in Kentucky.

Jeff Simonson – Mary's youngest son lives in Florida.

Bonny Knaack – Jeff's partner, is a nurse.

Liza Woitas – my helper, Liza. She does everything and anything I ask her to do, comes here three times a week for a couple hours, and more if I need her.

Ellen Matzke – my neighbor six doors down the street that stops almost every day, always with some goodies.

Maura Randall-Kutcher – comes often. She was the administrator of the grieving section of hospice. She started to come here shortly after Lydia died and still comes even though she has changed jobs and works at the state hospital now, and isn't obligated in any way. She's a real professional for sure. Her husband, Greg Kutcher, is a medical doctor. They have three girls. One through with college, one in college, and one senior in High School. Super people.

Caroline and Harold Dougherty – Caroline is a daughter of Lydia's older sister, Valeria. Harold comes here real often to chew the fat and have a short one. They practically feed me. They're so generous.

Daisy Schmidt – my sister, lives by a lake north of Park Rapids, MN.

Norton Schmidt – her husband, is deceased.

Tom Stone – my brother, lives in Rainier, Washington with his wife, Nita

Richard (Dick) Footner – my brother, deceased. Doris Footner- his wife deceased.

Wes Cornish and Jess Cornish – I was in the CCC camp with Wes in 1934. They've remained good friends over the years. Super people. Irene Cornish – Wes's wife, passed away shortly after Lydia did.

Mike Cornish – Wes's son. He comes to visit quite often.

Dorothy Peterson – good neighbor four doors down the street. She has taken me to church since Lydia passed away.

Inez and Lois Wilson – good friends from high school. We still keep in touch.

Art – my first Seeing Eye dog.

Milo – my second Seeing Eye dog.

ACKNOWLEDGMENTS

I want to thank those people who helped me write this biography, especially Larry Hutson, who listened to my tapes and organized my story.

I also want to express my deep appreciation to my good friend Maura, who transcribed all my tapes, posed the interview questions, facilitated the recordings, mailed packages, read and reread the many drafts and did a thousand other things for this biography.

I want to thank my "draft" readers: Verdi, Ellen, Liza and Holly. Your time and effort is much appreciated.

I want to thank my daughter, Mary, for her hard work, for finding Larry and the Publisher on her computer, for all the hundreds of email correspondence and for putting the polish on the finished product.

I also want to express my appreciation to all those family and friends who encouraged me along the way. Thank you to all of you.

Harry

APPENDIX

1

THE MORGAN MESSENGER, MORGAN MINNESOTA 1940

HARRY FOOTNER NOW CAN FACE ANY TRAFFIC HAZARD WITH NEW FRIEND

Art, Seeing Eye dog to provide sight for new master; fourth in state

Harry Footner is one happy man these days, as he became the owner of a Seeing Eye dog.

Harry returned last week from Morristown, New Jersey, where he underwent a month's training with his dog Art. They reside in Mankato but have been visiting here at Morgan this week.

Harry is a nephew of Mrs. Eli Lamp and a brother of Daisy Footner, both of Morgan.

More than three years ago Mr. Footner had the misfortune to lose his eyesight. He has been able to accommodate himself to his new life in everything but traffic hazards which provide danger enough for any of us. This is where Art fits in.

Standing quietly by his master in the picture the German shepherd dog is indeed an accomplished guide. Acting as eyes for Footner, Art watches traffic, warns of obstacles on the sidewalk and becomes a part of the master.

The dog is one of the German shepherds trained by the Seeing Eye Inc., which has been operating since 1929 in Morristown, New Jersey. For three months the dog went through intensive training so thorough that no hazard is too difficult for him to overcome.

The training does not stop with the dog. The master too must become accustomed to his dog and the dog to his charge. Part of the training included walking through heavy New York City traffic. After that both are ready to face the severe tests that are many times met at home.

Art is one of four Seeing Eye dogs in Minnesota, which gives Harry and his new pal more of a distinction than ever. Another coincidence is the fact that both Harry and Art can celebrate their birthday on the same day, June 19.

From now on the two of them will share the same experiences. The three-year-old dog spends 24 hours a day with his master and is never separated.

Mr. Footner spends a good deal of his spare time reading via the phonograph on which books have been recorded and thus can be played. He can also make some use of the Braille system. Harry cannot be lost in Mankato even in a car. He always knows just where he is at and can find his way around Morgan when he visit's the Lamp family even though he has not lived here for long periods of time.

2

MANKATO FREE PRESS 1942

SEEING EYE DOG MAKES HIT AT BUREAU MEETING

Garden City, February 20

"Art", the Seeing Eye German shepherd dog, made a decided "hit" at the regular Farm Bureau meeting at the school house on Monday night, in Garden City, when he appeared in person with his master, Harry Footner of Mankato, who has been blind for four years, through an accident.

"One of the greatest thrills of my life, Footner said in his talk, "was when my hat was brushed from my head by an awning, I didn't know where it fell, but when I told Art to "fetch" and unleashed him, in a minute he was back with my hat – that was the supreme thrill of my life, because I knew I was safe with Art as long as he was with me – he was really my eyes."

Continuing, Footner told of his course at "Seeing Eye" school in Morristown N. J., in preparation to taking this dog as a guide, where dog and master must both go through a strict training course to be certain that dog and master are well suited to each other.

Footner held his audience in close attention as he told of his experiences with his Seeing Eye dog, who has become such an important part of his master's life.

3

MANKATO FREE PRESS 1942

THIS 'N' THAT BY MARGE

One of the most unusual and best Farm Bureau programs, we have ever attended, was given at the local meeting, last night – and we have attended several, over a period of years – it was not that so much time was spent in preparing the program for the evenings entertainment, but the fact that the committee had a good drawing-card in the shape of a dog that was the highlight of the evening, and we all know that an intelligent dog, friend of man – and small boys – as an interest "getter-upper" is hard to beat.

So when Harry Footner, of Mankato – a young chap who lost his eyesight about four years ago, through an accident, appeared at the school-auditorium, with "Art" his "Seeing Eye" dog as guide, every youngster as well as oldster, immediately became curious to see and hear about this marvelous dog, who takes his master any place that any sighted person can travel, and who has become more necessary and vital than anything else could possibly be, to this man.

Of course we have all read of the "Seeing Eye" school at Morristown, New Jersey, which trains and provides dogs as guides for blind people – but many of us had not the pleasure of seeing one in action.

When an application for a dog from this school, is accepted, according to Mr. Footner, then that person must attend this school for a period of training and observation. Each student is studied for several days to find the type of dog that would be suitable for that particular man – or woman – for there are lady students as well as men – then the class is assembled in one room, given some hamburger, and one dog is brought into the room, this dog goes from hand to hand smelling the meat, and finally returns to one person and eats the meat from his hand – and that act, decides who his master shall be from now on.

Prior to this, the student has been training in the methods of following and giving orders to the dog he will receive when he has become efficient along that line – and the teacher trainer places a dog's harness over his arm and leads the student about the yards, streets and for hikes as would the regular guide dog, with the student giving the commands and learning to overcome the timidness about taking steps which is only natural to any person who cannot see just where he is going.

These students are under observation at all times, they do not know just where nor how close the trainer keeps to them.

The physical and mental health go far towards helping these students through the strict course of training they must have before they are allowed to leave school with the dog as their "seeing eye".

Some of the students are too nervous to become a good and efficient master for a "Seeing Eye" dog, and sometimes they have not the willpower, due to their blindness, to finish the course, which usually lasts from four to 16 weeks, depending upon the ability of the student to advance.

Barriers are placed about the grounds, for the dogs to guide their masters around, boxes, benches, holes, pipes, brush, puddles and spots of ice are all used to train the student and dog for any kind of a situation that may ever come up – all these under the trainers eye, so that he may know these two – the man and the dog will be able to cope with anything that arises.

Crossing the streets in traffic is one of the hardest parts of the training, first they are taken to a place where there is hardly any traffic and taught how to cross the street safely, the dog must stop when he comes to the curb, then at the command of his master, he goes across – unless there is a car coming – if so, he refuses to move, and the master wait's a minute and listens – for he must know from the sounds which we people with eyes so often miss – what is causing the delay, and from there to the heaviest traffic, and you may be sure he has complete confidence in his dog's judgment – then when the street is clear, the dog leads his master across.

The dog stays close to his master at all times, and is fed twice a day, two pounds of a prepared dog food and two pounds of dog biscuits, with a bone to enjoy once a week and no one is supposed to pet or make over this dog, other than his master.

An hour passed by very quickly as we listened to Mr. Footner's talk, and as he invited questions many more interesting incidents and facts were told us. The youngsters sat spellbound through the whole thing – and you must know – if you have ever been around boys, how hard it is to sit still, that this feature of our Farm Bureau program was worth a lot of any mans time – to any of us.

Pity changed to admiration, for this mans ability to learn a trade and support himself by piano tuning, even though he is blind, even though he must have gone through agony such as few of us have ever seen to take his place in life – as he told us simply and sincerely how he depended upon his dog to take him through the thickest traffic – if needs be – in fact to be a "Seeing Eye" for him.

So if you feel you have more that your load to carry, just get your Farm Bureau to contact this man, and give him a place on your program, or the 4-H club, he will fit into any group, and we are sure you will enjoy it more than you think you possibly could – its something that stays with you for several days, and we folks that have all our eyes, ears, hands and feet, brains and health have no reason to complain. We won't, ever, after hearing and seeing this man and his dog.

4

MANKATO FREE PRESS 1942

HANDICAPPED WORKERS DO BIT FOR ALLIED VICTORY BY BEN DETERMAN

Harry Footner, Accompanied by Seeing Eye Dog, Works at Automatic Electric; Don Bateman Works at Home

Harry Footner, totally blind, from an accident he suffered 10 years ago, and Donald Bateman, paralyzed from his hips down, are making a place for themselves in the work toward victory at the Automatic Electric Company.

Footner, with the help of his Seeing Eye dog, Art, has been working at Automatic Electric Company shops since December. He has been assigned work throughout the plant, on various processes and machines, and according to his foreman, Ray Schneider, has consistently turned out work well above average. He sits at his drill press during the eight-hour shift with his Seeing Eye companion at his feet. His fingers nimbly pick up the various components, place them together and work them into the machine until at the end of his work period; he has done well over the average quota of work. His touch has developed to a degree that he can gauge tolerances to the thousands of an inch merely by moving his fingers over the finished product. Footner, modestly speaking of his duties, turned the conversation to that of his constant companion. "Art has given me a new confidence in myself," said Footner, "he has long ago ceased to be an animal and became a part of me, bringing me safely to and from work, anticipating all my desires while I am here working and guiding me through the crowded workroom without difficulty."

Donald Bateman, injured in a motorcycle accident five years ago, when his machine toppled over on him in a hill climbing contest, breaking his back and leaving him paralyzed from his hips down, cheerfully insists that he is merely continuing work that he began even before he was called upon to do war work. Busy in his cycle repair shop in the rear of his home at 231 Mound Avenue, Bateman says that he would much rather work than loaf and lie around. He had just recently finished a huge order of many thousand resistor coils for the Automatic Electric Company and was, as he said, "taking things easy" by repairing several motorcycles which were in the shop.

The workshop is a veritable miracle land with ingenious devices crammed into every corner. In the production of the resistor coils he devised a method of power winding, which in addition to properly guiding the resistance wire on a clay core, provides an automatic counter on two operations. In this way the production was almost doubled, and the quality of the work was more accurate and uniform. In addition to this he made himself a chair scooter, which provides him with locomotion around the shop. His workbenches are cut low so he can work at them while sitting on the scooter. Another device is a frame, which will allow him to stand at his work where the operation demands this position.

5

MANKATO FREE PRESS MARCH 1, 1945

1,300 ATTEND 'E' AWARD CEREMONY AT ARMORY

*Automatic Electric Wins Army and Navy Praise for War Production; Blind
Employee Gets Special Recognition*

The first 'E' pennant won by a Mankato war plant flew over the Automatic Electric Manufacturing Company at 10 State Street today, following ceremonies last night at the Armory, when a crowd of 1,300 saw army and navy officials present awards to the firm's management and employees.

The pennant was hung above the Automatic Electric plant this morning at 8:30 as both officials and employees of the company resumed the work that has won praise from the navy and war departments. The award is made for efficiency in producing war materials.

Singled out for special recognition when the award was presented, were Harry Footner, 30-year-old blind employee, and his Seeing Eye dog, "Art".

After Lieutenant Colonel J. W. Homewood had tendered lapel pins for the firm's almost 180 employees, Footner and his dog marched to the front of the Mankato Armory stage.

The colonel, in giving a pin to Footner, commended him for overcoming "life's greatest handicap." the young man, who has been employed at Automatic for about a year and a half, doing precision work, lost his sight in an accident eight years ago.

For Art, the soft-spoken army officer had a silver badge with the words "E award" and the dog's name on it, to be worn on his collar. Art carefully guides his master to and from the plant and sits patiently by while he works, the colonel related.

Climax of the presentation ceremony at the Mankato Armory was the moment when Naval Captain George F. Jacobs of Minneapolis, inspector of navy ordnance and material, handed J. Fred Krost, manager of Automatic, the swallow-tailed, brightly-colored "E" pennant.

He called Automatic the defense plant that began as a "hobby", apparently referring to the origin of the firm in Krost's passion for tinkering with electrical time switches more than a quarter of a century ago.

Krost, in accepting the pennant called this event "the happiest moment of my life." he attributed the honor to "the individual effort of every man and woman employed in our company."

Then, after the third regimental state guard band had burst into "Anchors Aweigh," the four-man color guard from the naval air station at Wold-Chamberlain field raised the pennant. The large audience stood as the flag climbed into the air.

When Colonel Homewood, director of supply at Fort Snelling awarded the army-navy "E" lapel pins for the almost 180 employees, a short acceptance speech was given by Ray Schneider on behalf of his fellow workers. Standing with Schneider at the microphone was a woman worker, Grace Heiser.

Master of ceremonies at the program was Lee Fisher, who gave brief biographies of the military officers as he introduced them. At the start of the program he introduced the company officials and the special guests, including Mayor C. K. Mayer. Krost's two partners, his wife and R. F. Krost, were presented.

In front of the stage were dozens of baskets of flowers that had been sent to the company. Adding to the splendor of the event were the usherettes who escorted guests to their seats in long flowing gowns.

After the formal presentation ceremony, the Armory was thrown into darkness and two war films were shown. Later a dance for the employees was held, to the rhythms of Spike Haskell.

This is the first "E" flag to float above a Mankato defense plant, although Mason City Tent and Awning Company, which is establishing a local branch here, has been awarded three pennants. The nearest firm outside the city to have received the honor is E. F. Johnson Company at Waseca.

ISBN 1-41204591-6

9 781412 045919